SAVE OUR SCHOOLS

SAVE OUR SCHOOLS

66 THINGS YOU CAN DO TO IMPROVE YOUR SCHOOL WITHOUT SPENDING AN EXTRA PENNY

A Guide for Parents & Everyone Concerned About the Education of Our Children

MARY SUSAN MILLER, PH.D.

HarperSanFrancisco
A Division of HarperCollins*Publishers*

FIRST EDITION

TEXT DESIGN BY IRENE IMFELD

Library of Congress Cataloging-in-Publication Data

Miller, Mary Susan.
  Save our schools : 66 things you can do to improve your school without spending an extra penny : a guide for parents & everyone concerned about the education of our children / Mary Susan Miller. — 1st ed.
      p.   cm.
  ISBN 0–06–250733–8 (alk. paper)
  1. School improvement programs—United States. 2. Home and school—United States. 3. Education—United States—Parent participation. 4. School management and organization—United States. I. Title
LB2822.82.M55 1993
371.2'00973—dc20   92—56416
                                                              CIP

93 94 95 96 97 ❖ RRD(H) 10 9 8 7 6 5 4 3 2 1

To Victoria Pryor, with thanks and affection

Contents

Introduction *ix*

I. What Parents Can Do *1*

II. How You Can Help Students
Become Part of the Solution *21*

III. How You Can Strengthen Teaching *37*

IV. How You Can Strengthen
Administration *89*

V. How You Can Involve Your
Community *145*

Introduction

American schools are in a mess. If you don't already know
this, just take a look at the bleak statistics that have emerged
over the past ten years. Kids simply aren't learning. They are
pulling down more A's and B's than ever before because of
inflated grades, but they're not getting an education. They
can't organize a paragraph (much less an essay); identify
Winston Churchill (much less Charlemagne); read Dickens
(much less Shakespeare); understand main ideas in a text
(much less infer meanings); separate major issues in a political campaign (much less handle their ambiguity); name the
capital of Germany (much less find Iraq on a map); or calculate percentages (much less figure out the cost per item in
the supermarket). Besides, SATs and comprehension scores
are falling; truancy and dropout rates are rising; and our
unanswered cries for help are getting louder.

One of the most touted reasons for our schools' poor
report card is a lack of funds, but despite its role as the fall
guy, the scarcity of money may not be the chief reason. I'll
admit we'd probably get better teachers if we could pay
them corporate salaries; kids would be more apt to do their
work if we didn't crowd them into big classes; the building
would be cleaner if we could pay for extra janitorial help; art
and music would stay in the curriculum if we didn't have to
cut the faculty budget; absences would drop if we could pay
additional office staff to check them out; bright kids would
be challenged and weaker ones reinforced if we could hire
tutorial aides. Obviously, money would improve our schools,
but we can't count on its being forthcoming.

Sure, it would be great if more money were devoted to
education, and it might be forthcoming with the new administration in Washington and the impact of books like

Jonathan Kozol's *Savage Inequalities*. But we can't simply wait for more money to come to our schools and count on its providing everything that's needed. I agree with the bumper sticker that says: "It will be a great day when our schools get all the money they need, and the Pentagon has to hold a bake sale to buy a bomber," but that day is not here yet. There are many things we can do now before that mythical day comes, and even if and when there's more money, these things are still vital to making education truly thrive. Money is only one part of the answer. Many cost-free changes can solve problems, and schools are initiating them through real involvement from parents, kids, teachers, administrators, and the community.

So the real reason for the failure of our schools lies not in absent dollars, but in our own willingness to sit around in despair. While we adults complain—and it's all of us, parents, teachers, students, administrators, and the whole disgruntled community—children continue to be poorly educated. Hundreds of thousands of kids are out there who can't read or write or compute above an elementary school level and who haven't been taught to think at all. Twenty-five years ago I taught seventh grade—grammar and outlining, unified and coherent writing, and reading for meaning; today I'm teaching the same thing to freshmen and sophomores in college, most of whom don't even know what I'm talking about.

Our schools don't have to be this bad. We can stop laying the blame on money and start looking for solutions within the budgets we have; we can solve our own school problems. By *we* I don't mean the other guy; I mean all of us, because what happens in our schools today determines what happens in our world tomorrow.

"No more kids down the drain," a principal I know promised parents at the last PTA meeting of the school year. With a summer of reorganizing and planning and studying, he revamped the school program and kept his word; without an extra penny from the city, state, or national coffers, he turned his school around. And he is not alone. Tucked away in pockets throughout the country are schools in which wonderful things are happening. Pennies from heaven haven't rained into their budgets, but they have found ways to work around the shortfall. They have better teachers, smaller classes, and cleaner buildings; they keep art and music in the curriculum; they cut truancy and absences; they challenge bright kids and reinforce weaker ones—without getting extra money. Teachers are teaching, and children are learning again—in small towns in Oklahoma and Colorado, Indiana and South Dakota, Tennessee and Vermont; in big cities like New York and Los Angeles; in rural areas and suburbs and inner cities. I have sat in those classrooms; I have talked to those parents, teachers, students, principals, businesspeople, and community leaders; I have read tales of the magic they make. They're proud and they're excited, because they know their kids are learning.

"But I'm only a parent. What can I do?" Don't say it. You are a *parent*—not *only* a parent. Your taxes pay for schools; children like yours fill schools; your vote elects the legislators, the board of education, and in many cases the superintendents who control schools. Your voice is loud. All you have to do is use it. In my last book, *The School Book: Everything Parents Must Know About Education,* I showed you how to improve your child's experience in school. In this book, I show you how to improve the school itself. You, too, can be proud and excited. You, too, can promise, "No more kids down the drain." You, too, can take specific steps to bring learning back into the classroom without additional money.

- Some of the steps you take will enable teachers to do a better job with the large classes they're stuck with.

- Some will provide the extra help individual students need.

- Some will enrich a watered-down curriculum.

- Some will eliminate graffiti.

- Some will let quick learners speed ahead.

- Some will cut down the dropout and absence rate.

- Some will put you, the parents, on the teaching team.

- Some will challenge unmotivated students.

- Some will raise school spirit.

- Some will get the community working for you.

- Some will even raise the school's test scores.

- All of these steps will release funds from nonessentials so they can be used for actual learning—and you'll feel as if you had indeed brought in extra dollars.

- And none of them will cost the school an extra penny, because the money you save by taking some steps can be spent in taking others.

All sixty-six of the following suggestions for improving your school are tried-and-true. I have initiated many of them myself, as a parent, as a teacher, as a principal; I have seen school personnel use some and community businesses and organizations use others in schools all over the country; I have watched students enthusiastically use them. You can use them, too; after all, most of them arose because parents cried, "Enough!" Give them a try. What have you got to lose? Better still, just think of all you have to gain.

PART I
What Parents Can Do

1 Make your PTA or parents' organization a power-house.

WHY?

Parent groups have clout. Let's face it, schools have a lot more parents than teachers and administrators, and it's you parents whose children are the focus of the whole system anyway. So don't be content with making cookies for the bake sale. If you think your child isn't getting the education he deserves, sound your voice and flex your muscle through an organized parent group. You'd be amazed at how parents have turned schools around: in California, for instance, they forced the board of education to lower a salary increase for teachers that would have necessitated cutbacks in curriculum, and in New York they got rid of a principal; in a sub-standard rural midwestern elementary school they demanded that all new teachers have certification and that those already on the faculty take courses to acquire it; in Chicago they succeeded in reinstating junior high art and science. Parent groups have banished junk food from the cafeteria and installed safety pads under the playground equipment. Whether your school has a parent-teacher association or a parents' organization, activate it and become a partner in power.

Although parents' organizations tend to remain localized, they bring the force of a school's parent body to bear on issues of concern. PTAs, on the other hand, belong to a network that ranges from individual school PTAs, through regional and state PTAs, and up to the national PTA. The national PTA not only keeps schools abreast of issues through publications and annual conferences but also lobbies in state capitals and in Washington, where it has played a major role in drug and sex-education legislation.

HOW?

- ✦ Send a charge through your next parent meeting by speaking up and saying what's on your mind. If you are displeased with the school, say why and ask other parents how they feel. Form a group to investigate and draw up some possible courses of action. The trouble with America's PTAs and POs is that only 25 percent of parents bother to attend meetings because they feel they have no point. Give your meeting a point—a sharp one.

- Join a committee; become the chairperson. If your time is limited because of a job, schedule meetings in the evening or on weekends; set a closing hour, and keep to your agenda to avoid wasteful chatter.

- Get yourself elected to office. As part of the organization's structure, you have power to put pressure not only on your school, but on the district as well. That's where change takes place.

- Do your homework before pushing for change. Present solid arguments and examples from other schools; gather facts and figures that the administrators will listen to. If you confront them with nothing but anger and sob stories, they'll just shrug you off as another complainer.

- Once you're in a position to recharge the parent group, recharge it. Start a membership drive. Bring in speakers parents want to hear. Tackle the troublesome areas in your school. Put all that parent power to work for a better school.

2 *Get into the school as a volunteer. School and college faculty and staff experienced mass firings in the 1992–93 school year—six thousand personnel in New York alone. You and other parents have the person-power to fill the gaps that are cheating your kids of learning. About 50 percent of America's parents give some kind of volunteer time to their children's school; you can bring that figure closer to 100 percent.*

WHY?

Two reasons. First, over fifty research studies show that your child's achievement will be higher if you're involved. It makes sense: when a child sees that school is important to a parent, school becomes important to him, too. Second, the work you do as a volunteer frees up money the school would have to pay an employee, releasing that money so it can be spent on teachers and programs the school couldn't otherwise afford. When you give time and energy as a volunteer, you're not just helping the school; you're helping your own child.

In the Stuart-Hobson School in Washington, D.C., for instance, when courses were about to be dropped for lack of funds, parents actually got into the classrooms and taught. In New York City schools, parents patrol the halls, staff libraries, tutor, and staff special programs; in P.S. 87 on the city's Upper East Side, on any given day twenty or more parents can be seen at work from helping in the library to assisting with bus departures, and they have had such success that at what was once a mediocre school at best, the principal is turning away student applicants by the hundreds. In Norwalk, Connecticut, one mother who believes that "when something looks wrong, it feeds decay" got parents to spruce up the whole school building, from the gym they painted green to the entrance to the student art gallery they redecorated. In Danville, Illinois, parents aid at-risk children by helping them with homework in an after-school program. One parent at Roosevelt School Primary Education Center in Redwood City, California, who introduced kids in kindergarten through sixth grade to Shakespeare, is now recognized in the community as "the Shakespeare Lady"; another parent at the same school, alarmed at the lack of an art program, developed and taught one. So vital are parents to the success of today's schools that the San Francisco Unified School District has a comprehensive parent-involvement policy. As the principal of Cardinal Ritter College Prep in St. Louis says, "If you're not going to be involved, maybe your children shouldn't be here."

HOW?

Develop a parent-volunteer committee to work with the school principal. Be positive, not belligerent, and assure her that volunteers will cooperate with the school, supplementing and supporting the program wherever she or they see a need. Give the principal a list of suggested areas where volunteers could help and let her, with input from students and faculty, come up with a list, too. Schools across the country are using parent volunteers in myriad ways:

- To phone home whenever a child is absent. Volunteers cut down on truancy and unauthorized absences by almost 90 percent.

- To tutor in the classroom. Volunteers give extra help to children who would otherwise fail, saving both the children and the school's reputation. Little Rock, Arkansas, reports great success, especially with at-risk children.

- To supervise the lunchroom. This is a rough job, and it takes a tough mom or dad to do it, but it lets the teacher previously assigned to the duty attend to what he's trained to do: teach the kids.

- To help out in the office by answering phones, taking messages, and stuffing envelopes. Volunteers enable the school to cut the cost of office staff and shift the dollars into education.

- To supervise students coming to school in the morning and leaving at dismissal time. By giving teachers a needed break from door and bus duty, volunteers raise teachers' morale and, as a result, their teaching level.

↜ To present assembly programs. Volunteers can draw on the talent and experience in the parent body to enrich students' learning in areas that include music, science, drug-abuse prevention, travel, the environment, politics, sports, and multicultural understanding. I used this idea to great advantage when I was a principal in Brooklyn in classes and assemblies for all grades.

↜ To help with special events such as parties, trips, sports events, fairs, and play productions. As a parent, you're probably doing plenty of this already, without realizing that you are also freeing a teacher to go home and correct papers.

↜ To serve as a class ombudsman, maintaining an open line of communication between parents and the teacher, listening to and filtering complaints. An ombudsman can on one side spare teachers unjustified frontal attacks, and on the other help parents express bona fide concerns.

3 When you schedule a teacher conference, make sure your child is there, too.

WHY?

If just you and the teacher sit down to discuss a problem, you're groping for solutions in the dark. The teacher will tell you what she sees; you'll relay what your child sees or wants you to see; and each of you will come away with only a piece of the picture. You won't know who's telling the truth. On the other hand, when all three of you sit down together, you get the facts firsthand, with no room for the old "He said that you said that he said . . . " buck-passing.

There's a long-term value, too. Psychiatrists feel that over-protection of a child leads to warped development as surely as does neglect. Personally, I view overprotection as a form of neglect, since overprotective parents neglect to give their children a chance to build coping skills. If you go alone to your child's teacher to solve problems when they arise, you make things smooth for him for a couple of days or weeks, but you also prepare a bumpy road for him down the years. On the other hand, if you and your child face the teacher together, and you limit your role to supporting him as he discusses the problem, handles the conflict, and works toward a resolution, you give him the gift of capability, from which stems the even greater gift of self-esteem. Your child will learn how to face a problem and accept it as his, not someone else's, and will be able to go through life confident he can solve any problems that come his way.

HOW?

Just do it. If the teacher balks, insist. If your child balks, insist. Studies show that kids are far more able to handle difficulties, even tragedy, than adults give them credit for; as a matter of fact, they are far more able than are many adults themselves. As a teacher, I insisted on three-way conferences and found a good many more compatible solutions than did my associates who went the traditional route. As a principal, I introduced the process with only two teachers willing to give it a try, but before the semester was out the whole fac-ulty—with a few holdouts—had come on board. And as a parent, I found that when my children ran into problems in school, three-way conferences enabled them to be far less defensive and more open to finding solutions.

Don't wait till there's a problem to set up a teacher conference. Go in with your child at the start of the year to meet the teacher. Express your deep interest in the school and in your child's education; offer to help; urge the teacher to keep in close touch with you. It is shocking to realize that according to a recent Maryland study, over a third of the parents surveyed had not met with a teacher during the year and close to two-thirds had not talked to a teacher by phone. Give your child a better chance by getting full value from teacher conferences.

4 *Read, read, read to your kids.*

WHY?

Dr. Ernest Boyer, president of the Carnegie Foundation for the Advancement of Teaching, has written a book called *Ready to Learn: A Mandate for the Nation,* in which he expresses his belief that the real test of learning readiness—before kindergarten, and later on as well—is language ability. "In order to strengthen learning," he writes, "first comes love, then language. . . . It's what good parenting is all about."

Studies show that children who are read to become readers. It's that simple. Why do you want your kid to be a reader? Because studies also show that readers tackle their schoolwork intelligently—understand, follow directions, use their imagination, write coherently, dig beneath words into meanings, think. In short, they have the verbal skills that lead to achievement. There's an added bonus, too: kids who read don't watch endless hours of television, which ongoing studies relate to poor school performance. Although dozens of studies within the last decade have confirmed that positive results occur when children read and are read to, teachers don't need to be convinced by studies: they see evidence every day in the classroom.

Reading and telling stories to young children lays the foundation of verbal skills upon which all future learning depends. Yet Dr. Boyer's book reports that a majority of kindergarten teachers find four of every ten children so deficient in verbal skills as to be classified "inadequately prepared to learn." The public school system in Comstock, Michigan, considers reading to children so vital that it has worked out a program with the local hospital that presents each mother of a newborn with a children's book and a letter explaining the importance of reading to one's child. Jim Trelease of the Center for the Study of Reading at the University of Illinois leaves little room for doubt when he says, "Reading aloud to children is the single most important activity contributing to their eventual success in school."

HOW?

- Start reading to your baby as soon as she can sit in your lap, round about five months. Get books with bright colors and pretty pictures; books with plenty of faces in them are particularly good. Although the words won't make sense to her, the excitement of the pages and the comfort of your voice and body will make an early connection in her between reading and pleasure. Verbalization develops in children as they hear voices speaking to them. Since being read to combines the visual with the aural, along with pleasurable body contact, it lays the cornerstone of speech from many dimensions.

- As your child becomes older, go to the library with her so that you can select books together. Set aside a time each evening for reading. She will look forward to it and find comfort in the bedtime routine. It has been found that even troubled children in juvenile detention homes relax and sleep better when read to at bedtime.

- When your child is able to read on her own, continue reading to her, but let her read to you, too. By being a partner in the fun, she will gain self-confidence.

- By the time your child enters sixth grade, reading will be a habit in your home. Now is the time to turn to the children's classics often ignored in schools—works by Robert Louis Stevenson and Louisa May Alcott, the Narnia books by C. S. Lewis, for example—and read a chapter a night, with the whole family taking turns. I used to let my children stay up an extra half hour at night to read in bed if they wanted to. It's a good way to foster reading, since kids will do almost anything to keep the light on; and if the reading avidity of my children (and their children) today is any indication, it works.

- Don't be afraid to let your teenagers read some current fiction. Eliminate the bloodiest and scariest and sexiest, but realize that John LeCarré and Anne Tyler speak the language and the situations of today that will engross your child; that's far better than having them turned off by force-fed Dickens.

✦ Many movies that appear today are based on books, lots of them good books like *The Color Purple* and *The Accidental Tourist*. If your children want to see the movie, you might suggest that they read the book first so their mind can range beyond the director's. Even more movies appear in book form after the movie's release, though not always with great literary value (like *Big* and *Gremlins II*). I don't suggest urging your children to read these books, but if they have seen the movie and want to, there's no reason not to let them.

✦ Chrysler Corporation, in conjunction with the American Federation of Teachers and the Association for Supervision and Curriculum Development, has developed a program to help parents build reading into their regular family activities. For details on obtaining a free video and booklet, contact your local Chrysler-Plymouth, Dodge, or Jeep-Eagle dealer.

5 Make courses available for parents.

WHY?

With the change in American demographics over the last few decades, many schools find a large percentage of parents unable to read or speak English. Even though such parents may be literate in their native tongue, if they can't read and speak English, they can't help their kids much with reading or schoolwork. Many parent groups have initiated classes in English as a second language to overcome this problem, and early results in Oklahoma indicate a three-pronged benefit: parents become more active in school affairs; teachers don't feel they have to shoulder the whole burden of non-English-speaking children; and children raise their achievement levels.

HOW?

Schools all over the country offer courses and workshops to meet other parent needs, recognizing that the more knowledgeable and secure parents are, the more they will be able to reinforce their child's learning. Some schools, like those in Jersey City, New Jersey, actually teach parents the basic skills they need to help their children at home. In some states, among them New Mexico and Pennsylvania, schools conduct workshops to teach parents the importance of self-esteem to their children and to give them guidelines for new methods of counseling and discipline.

Fifteen years ago, Ernest Boyer, then U.S. commissioner of education, introduced the idea that "since home is the first school, parents should be helped in their role as teachers." Last year the New York City Board of Education took up the cry with twenty-five hundred parents in a workshop called "Parents as Partners in Education, from A to Z." Schools and districts throughout the state are following through at the local level.

Interviews with parents, with teachers and administrators, and with students—after all, they're the ones who have to cope with their parents' problems—may reveal some crying needs among parents that your PTA or PO can meet. Send out a questionnaire. When you tabulate the results, find volunteers among the parent group or in the community to develop classes or workshops to address the needs that emerge.

6 *Stop taking responsibility for your child's homework. It's his; let him decide to do it . . . or not do it.*

WHY?

Taking on responsibility gives children the coping skills required for wise decision making. The baby crawls and then stands up, determines to put one foot before the other, and takes a step. If her parents grab her, shouting, "No, you'll fall and hurt yourself," each time she tries, she'll never learn to walk. If they let her try, let her fall, and then comfort her and love her in her failure, she'll try again and soon succeed.

Doing homework is a step a child must take for himself, although reasons for not doing it are never in short supply: "I want to watch TV"; "I'm afraid I'll get it wrong"; "I'll do it later." Parents get caught up in a nighttime ritual of nagging, coaxing, screaming, punishing, and even doing the homework themselves. Why? Partly, they wear out. But even more, they can't bear for their child to face the failure of undone homework; it hurts their pride. By taking homework responsibility upon themselves, parents, while assuring their child of success in school the next day, also assure him of many pain-filled failures in the future when there is no one around to bear his burden. I know of more than one teenager who couldn't handle college work and had to leave because his parents were suddenly not there to nag him. "He always did it at home," one mother told me incredulously.

Only when a child is given the choice to do or not to do his homework will he learn that his decision has a consequence: if yes, his teacher's acceptance; if no, her displeasure and perhaps a stay after school, makeup work on Saturday, or a failing grade. When parents don't let him take the step of undone homework, it's true he won't fall on his face, but neither will he learn accountability for decisions—a fact that, as he gets older, will entail far more lethal consequences than undone homework.

Self-esteem grows from responsibility, the wonderful sense of "I can." So vital is self-esteem to healthy growth and learning that the Arkansas House of Representatives introduced a bill requiring teacher training in strategies that build self-esteem. The bill did not pass—not because the legislators considered self-esteem irrelevant, but because they considered it so integral a part of learning that they found a way more efficient than mandate to accomplish the same end: including it in teachers' college training. Parent programs in hundreds of schools reach for a similar goal, and parents in thousands of homes attain that goal by stepping back from their child's homework.

HOW?

Let your child know that his education is important to you. Provide him with a place where he can work—his own room, or the local library if home is too noisy and chaotic. Or, as recent studies indicate, perhaps he will feel less isolated and work better in the living room, with the family around him. Don't panic if he has the radio on: today's kids are less stressed out when they work to background music. However, once the scene is set, let him realize that learning is his business—that no one can do it for him, and no one is going to force him to do it. Be ready and willing to help in constructive ways if you're asked: listen to spelling words, explain a math problem, review history notes. Help, but don't *do*.

You have two jobs in this process. One is to back off and, if homework goes undone, let it happen without a scene. This is harder than it sounds, but remember, the decision to do homework is his, not yours. Your second job is to make sure the teacher doesn't let your child get away with not doing homework. If she is lax in following through, explain that in your family, homework is considered a child's job and turned completely over to him. If he chooses not to do it, you won't interfere, but you expect the teacher to hold the child accountable and the child to take the consequences. Dr. Robert Brooks, a psychology professor at Harvard Medical School, believes that children have to shoulder responsibility and face any ensuing mistakes and failures in order to avoid what he calls "learned helplessness." You can set your children on the path to learned self-sufficiency by refusing to let them give you homework.

7 Get your child to school. Don't let her fool you with "headaches" on test day, and don't write excuses that aren't true.

WHY?

First of all, your child can't learn if she isn't in school. With unbridled truancy as high as 33 percent in some areas, parents can keep their school's learning level up by keeping absences down.

Second, if you buy into her headache act by letting her skip school, you're giving her a hands-on lesson in the effectiveness of deception. When a feigned headache works once, why not try it twice? When a lie keeps her home from school, what greater ends might it not accomplish?

Third, if you accept a phony headache as her reason for wanting to avoid school, you will probably never learn the real reason. Maybe she's bored or scared of failing; maybe her classmates tease her; maybe the teacher scapegoats her; maybe she has a learning problem. Unless you find out, you can't deal with the problem and help her solve it.

Fourth, if your child gives in to every little headache— real or imagined—she is en route to becoming a hypochondriac, a syndrome that can cripple her activities for life. Let her know that you, she, and all of us learn to carry on with a little ache here or there, which usually goes away as we become absorbed in work or play. If the problem persists, that's another story, one to tell a doctor.

HOW?

When your child confronts you with a headache or stomachache before school, don't laugh it off, and don't accuse her of lying. Instead, listen and check: take her temperature; recall what she has eaten, when she has eliminated, what previous symptoms she may have shown, who else in the family has been sick. If you find no symptoms of sickness, tell her to go to school and see whether she doesn't feel better in an hour or so. If she is afraid she will be sick in school, give her a note asking the teacher to call you if she feels worse or to send her to the nurse. Chances are she'll forget all about her ache and fall into the swing of activities once she's at school.

On the other hand, if she's really sick, you'll hear from the nurse.

If headache manipulation persists, she is probably facing a difficulty at school with which she can't cope. Try to draw her out. A blunt "What's wrong, honey?" won't work; it's invasive. Try a more empathic "You seem upset. Won't it help to talk?" If that fails, you and she should talk to the teacher together, putting facts and feelings gently on the table.

8 When your child brings home complaints about a teacher, check them out rather than storming the classroom.

WHY?

Interviews indicate that over half of America's parents think teachers are unwelcoming, even hostile, to them, and my experience tells me they are right. When teachers see a parent descending upon them, they immediately set up battlements against an offensive they have learned to expect after years of accusations. Like many of us, teachers may decide that the best defense against a parent confrontation is a strategic attack of their own. "Jimmy says I hate him? Well let me tell you, Jimmy is the biggest troublemaker in class."

The cure, therefore, rests with parents: reach out with open palms, not with fists, when your child runs into trouble. Parents, teachers, and children have to realize that they are on the same team, aiming to make the same goal, if a school is going to work for any of them. Your attitude in handling difficult times with your child and his teacher will go a long way toward scoring that goal.

HOW?

"My teacher picks on me"; "My teacher doesn't explain"; "My teacher isn't fair"; "My teacher gives too much homework." When you hear these familiar refrains, instead of rising like a tiger to defend her cub, ask your kid what the teacher specifically said or did; get the facts. Then try to find out what your kid specifically said or did to set the scene. What was he doing, what were his classmates doing, that might have angered the teacher? Don't accept generalities such as "She's mean" or "She hates me," because they're opinions, not the facts you need to size up the situation. You want to know whether the children were talking or giggling or passing notes.

If it turns out that your child's own behavior has caused the teacher to be what your child considers unfair, give him a lesson in cause and effect, a great teachable moment to grasp. If, however, you get the feeling that the teacher really has acted unjustly, make an appointment for the two of you to see her. But don't go in with your fists up; the approach I have seen work best begins, "We seem to have a problem here. Let's see what the three of us can do to solve it."

By working constructively with a teacher, you are in a position to raise the education level of both your school and your child. But keep a few things in mind:

- Teachers are only human: just like you, they get frustrated and hurt and angry and defensive.

- Arguments have two sides—your child's and the teacher's. Hear them both.

- You and the teacher aren't on opposite sides. She wants your child to learn as much as you do.

In 1991 The Carnegie Foundation for the Advancement of Teaching published a report called *Ready to Learn: A Mandate for the Nation*. It is a checklist for parents, suggestions to help them equip their children—intellectually and emotionally—for the learning years ahead. The advice is so sound that I offer it here for parents and teachers too in the hope that children of all ages will not only begin school ready to learn, but will continue through the years ready, eager, and able:

- Keep the home a secure place for your children.
- Remember how much the surrounding language promotes learning.
- Read aloud regularly.
- Hug and hold.
- Listen and respond.
- Try for relaxed and gentle conversation.
- Avoid curt commands and careless responses.
- Find ways to surround them with books.
- Try for more ritual like the family meal.
- Help them understand the disconnected pieces of their lives.
- Feel better about yourself and you'll be a better parent [and teacher].
- Explore community programs designed to help parents do better.
- Be involved with school and all its activities.
- Remember you are the first and most essential teachers.
- Always love them a little more than you think they need.

PART II
How You Can Help Students Become Part of the Solution

9 *Make your children realize that if they're not part of the solution, they are part of the problem. Show them how to get involved; urge them to get in there and make change happen.*

WHY?

Students are the first ones to know when school isn't giving them what they need. But what do they do about it? You know: they complain or stop trying or cut classes or cover the school walls with graffiti and carve up the desks. Eventually they even drop out—over a third of them in some areas. Giving up doesn't change the school or improve their chances for a good education . . . a good job . . . a good life. Working within the system does. You as a parent can help your children and their classmates work within the system in order to make the system work for them.

HOW?

Your school probably has a student government—in name only and sadly inactive, if your school is like most. Well, activate it. Get a group of schoolmates who want more than they're getting to brainstorm and identify some specific problem areas—not teachers they hate or the need for a new gym, but new ways of teaching, new courses, new kinds of student involvement, more field trips, tutors for extra help, guidance sessions, honors classes—real learning improvements. Show your kids how to investigate problem areas by talking to other students and teachers and by checking out other schools. Help them back up their findings with solid evidence, so their arguments will convince the authorities instead of turning them off to what they may otherwise see as antiestablishment rebellion.

Get the PTA or PO to support student government, and set up a joint meeting—parents, students, faculty, and principal. Students have been catalysts for big changes in schools— from relaxing a dress code in Brooklyn and demanding a career-development course in Los Angeles to fighting crime in Tulsa. Students working actively for change acquire a con- fidence-building sense of control; students working construc- tively are taken seriously by the principal and teachers.

Although student involvement in school planning and operation is not new, it usually has no effect on core issues. Administrators tell me, "I'm afraid of what the kids will come up with." But the administrators at Walden III, an inner-city public school in Racine, Wisconsin, weren't afraid: students not only selected the school name but also set up a student government that votes equally with the faculty on matters ranging from grades to cheating and that calls a town meeting whenever an issue concerning the whole school arises. Does it work? The school started eighteen years ago and is stronger than ever today.

10 *Get students involved in a community-service program. If they demonstrate their commitment to it, suggest that they make a move to convince the principal to give it course credit.*

WHY?

Although volunteerism is as American as McDonald's, few children are given an opportunity to learn the rewards it offers. Of the approximately 1.35 million children engaged in volunteer work, two-thirds are in school-based programs, yet only a very few of the schools involved offer credit. At Fallston High School in Maryland, for instance, three hundred members of a school service club visit nursing homes, work in soup kitchens, and sponsor wheelchair basketball. Receiving neither course credit nor certificates of appreciation, they find other, more valuable rewards—primarily, the satisfaction of helping others. Studies, however, reveal more: children who do volunteer work improve their problem-solving and critical-thinking skills, as well as becoming more responsible. Volunteerism is a win-win situation for both donor and recipient.

HOW?

Since over half of school-based volunteer work is done through school clubs, an easy way for students to get started is to form a service club and decide what organizations in the neighborhood need them. To find this out, they should send small groups to nursing homes, hospitals, orphanages, social-service organizations, homes for the physically and/or mentally disabled, and so forth to talk to personnel, find out about the organizations' needs, and explain what the service club could do to help. Those students who shy away from personal contact should consider volunteering with parks, zoos, or environmental groups.

While most school-based volunteerism involves high school students, it can begin as early as primary school: I have seen first- and second-graders draw pictures and make baskets for the aged and the homeless. The energies of junior high students are particularly effective when directed to volunteer work: as a principal, I took seventh-graders to a nursing home once a week, where they enlivened bored TV-viewing patients with songs and stories. They felt good about it, but perhaps little realized that as they shed their giggles and gossip at the door, they became the most giving of adults.

Schools underscore the value of volunteer work when they acknowledge its importance with course credit. A teacher I know in Perry, Oklahoma, uses a local old-age home as an integral part of her third-grade teaching: students write letters to the old people and read their replies aloud in class. Several times a month they follow through with a visit; I almost cried when I saw their mutual joy as the old ears listened to the young voices. A middle school in Colorado Springs requires students in sixth through eighth grade to participate in a program called HUGSS (Helping Us Grow Through Service and Smiles), in which students take pets along on visits to senior citizens, play games with blind and deaf children, and recycle cans and newspapers, giving the proceeds to needy families. High school students in Atlanta, Georgia, who are required to give seventy-five hours of volunteer time in order to graduate, often end up giving as many as four hundred. The middle school of Norfolk Academy in Virginia Beach closes Wednesday afternoons so that every seventh-, eighth-, and ninth-grader can do community service—helping old people in a nursing home, perhaps, or weeding at the local botanical garden.

11 *Save the school money by organizing a rotating student cleanup committee. You can rouse enthusiasm by showing kids how the money they save can be used to buy programs or equipment they want but the school can't afford.*

WHY?

Walking through the school cafeteria one lunchtime, I saw a girl toss a paper cup on the floor. "Would you be good enough to put that in the wastebasket, please?" I asked her.

"Isn't that what we have janitors here for?" she countered.

I told her no, and she complained to her mother.

Since parents haven't done the job—and when you look at the litter on sidewalks and roadsides and in parks, you know they haven't—the school can help out by letting students know that maids, janitors, and custodians are not there to clean up after them. That is the students' own job. Furthermore, it has been shown—in my own school, for one—that when students have to pick up their own mess, they make less of it.

A cleanup crew is essential to education because a clean building in good repair is conducive to learning. When that condition can be maintained without heavy staff expenses, the money saved buys additional equipment, adds an extra course, or rewards a teacher for a job well done. Therefore, when students take on some of the work of the cleanup staff, they help themselves directly in two ways: they develop a sense of responsibility, and they buy themselves a better education.

HOW?

Student-government officers should begin by discussing their plan with the school principal. Let them do a good selling job, since he has to believe in the program strongly enough to reinforce it. With the principal's support well in place, the student government can appoint (or elect) a building committee to undertake a threefold job:

1 Decide what jobs the students are able to perform: picking up litter in the yard, halls, and classrooms; washing off or painting over graffiti; washing chalkboards. This should be determined in conjunction with the custodian.

2 Assign students to specific jobs and areas on a weekly basis.

3 Ascertain that the work is being done adequately.

I have personally seen this kind of program work in three schools and am both surprised and disappointed that more schools haven't taken the initiative. Why not see what your students can do with it?

12 *Encourage students to create a weekly newslet-*
ter covering their thoughts and concerns, to be circu-
lated among the school population. More editorially
focused and less newsy than the school newspaper (if
there is one), it keeps communications open and works
as an agent for change.

WHY?

The airing and sharing of ideas, worries, and gripes are
signs of health in a school—no festering sores, no circulating infections, a temperature of 98.6. A middle school English class in Ohio produced a weekly newsletter that served
as a catalyst for the whole school when a furor brewed over
a newly instituted dress code. Not only did the students in
the class voice the pros and cons of the issue as well as their
reactions, but they sent reporters to interview other students
and teachers, even the principal. When faced with the
results of these efforts, the principal agreed to a compromise.

The great student rebellion of the sixties began when students reached the explosion point over being mute; suddenly
voices on the Berkeley campus burst forth, inciting rage and
destruction that spread across the country. In the following
decade, high schools that downplayed or ignored the horror
students felt over Vietnam, Cambodia, and Kent State found
themselves confronted with demonstrations and violence.
Those that not only let students speak but listened to them,
as my school did, channeled the anger into student-faculty
teaching and learning.

Because it is immediate and because it requires thinking
and skill to produce, a weekly newsletter is the perfect vehi-
cle for student expression. To the relief of students, they can
say what's on their minds; to the relief of teachers, class
standards demand that the students say it well; and to the
relief of everyone, the school avoids revolution, which,
according to the former head of the Lakeside School in Seattle, "always means losing much of the good along with the
bad."

HOW?

The best way to start a student newsletter is to have an English teacher incorporate it as part of the writing program; in this way, the entire class participates. This has been done successfully in many elementary schools. Under the restrictive burden of curriculum and schedule requirements, junior and senior high schools most often produce a weekly newsletter, like the newspaper and yearbook, as an after-school club activity. This works, too, but it limits participation to far fewer students.

In either case, however, the supervising teacher, be it the English teacher or a faculty adviser, must run the newsletter on democratic principles, truly advising, not dictating. Together the teacher and students will outline rules—no obscenity, name-calling, or rumor-mongering; a commitment to accuracy and honest expression—and together they will see that the rules are adhered to. I have never heard of a school where a newsletter of this type did not reap rich rewards, but neither have I heard of one where a few parents and teachers haven't tried to undermine the newsletter through their own fears and lack of trust in student judgment. Be prepared, and your students will do a good job.

13 Get the student government to set up ongoing discussions with other schools on topics ranging from political issues to problems of education.

WHY?

Results of a recent study exploded like fireworks across the country, revealing that over 75 percent of high school students were unable to name their senators, about 66 percent were unable to define the Bill of Rights, and close to 85 percent were unable to name the leaders of four industrial countries. Students do not read newspapers or newsmagazines, nor do they watch the news on television; yet at eighteen they can vote. They are too busy with school, homework, an after-school job, and their weekend social life to get involved in national and world affairs, and schools have little time in the schedule to include what used to be called civics.

Therefore, it is up to students themselves to solve the problem, and one of the most successful and fun ways some of them have found to do this is to arrange discussions with other schools. Unlike debates, discussions of this kind follow no formula, nor are there teams and assigned topics. On the contrary, students from one school invite students from another for a general discussion of, perhaps, elections, the environment, foreign trade, or even controversial subjects such as sex education, abortion, and religious fundamentalism. When large numbers of students participate, they need to be divided into smaller groups so that everyone has a chance to talk. Eighth-graders at the Master's School in Dobbs Ferry, New York, found themselves discussing not only politics but plans for a joint dance at Christmas.

HOW?

Programs of this kind can be run by the student government or by a club—the Idea Exchange, as one school called its club. In either case, it should be students, not teachers, who decide who is to be invited, what the general subject matter is to be, and who is to be the adviser. The general consensus is that, when followed by dinner or an informal dance, discussions serve a welcome dual purpose.

14 *Don't stop there. Get students involved with their local government—addressing the mayor and city council about their concerns, working for candidates they support, drawing up proposals for change.*

WHY?

A recent Times Mirror survey reported on the apathy of young people toward public affairs, pointing out that far fewer eighteen- to twenty-four-year-olds vote, read newspapers, and even watch TV news than people aged twenty-five to fifty. The director of the study is pessimistic about the country's future because he sees the lack of political concern among the young not only continuing, but actually increasing.

Students are in a position to reactivate involvement in a world beyond school, home, and the shopping mall; and if teachers are not pulling the world into their classrooms, let students push themselves into the world. With many current issues affecting young people directly—AIDS, abortion, civil rights, poverty, clean air, education, elections—it's important to encourage them to become aware of issues and actions being taken. Get them to see that the quality of their lives depends, and will depend even more strongly in the future, on their ability to find solutions to and take action on the nation's problems.

HOW?

Work through the student government. Parents, teachers, administrators, even students themselves can give the initial push, but once they are in the real world, dealing with real issues, kids become—the magic word for educators—motivated! About five hundred high school students in Holyoke, Massachusetts, marched to city hall to protest the poor conditions in their school; the entire student body of an elementary school wrote letters to their senators and representatives prior to the clean-air vote; a group of middle schoolers volunteered to hand out campaign fliers for local Republican and Democratic clubs. If the director of Times Mirror surveys is right, when kids like these reach eighteen, political apathy should see a sharp turnaround.

15 *Work with the student body to provide pro-grams in areas where students have a need—an after-school tutoring program, like the one in Forestville, Maryland; a program for life-management skills, like the one in Largo, Florida; a summer literacy program, like the one in San Antonio, Texas; a support group for pregnant teens, like the one in Philadelphia.*

WHY?

Students know where their schools are failing them. What they don't know soundly enough, however, is what they can do about it. If you let them know that you care, that you are listening, and that you understand, you are halfway toward motivating them into action. The second half is convincing them they can fill in the school's gaps by meeting the admin-istration's "Sorry, we have no money" with a determined "Then we'll do it ourselves."

HOW?

Some student governments have surveyed their consitutents to determine what they think the needs are; others have held town meetings. In both cases they have taken the results to the principal and the parents, who together have figured out ways to implement the suggested programs, usually with the help of student, parent, and community volunteers.

16 *Impress on your child the importance of asking for extra help when she needs it.*

WHY?

Many children pick up the school's signal that weakness and failure are stigmas too shameful to be brought to light. As a result, a difficulty that could be rectified with ease early on becomes a looming problem crushing self-esteem and leading to defeat. According to the *Brown University Child Behavior and Development Letter,* the freedom to make mistakes is a path to healthy growth; the confidence that comes from correcting mistakes is a path to learning. Whether the help needed is academic or personal, early reaching out puts control in the child's hands, dispelling fears of inadequacy and helplessness.

HOW?

When an infant is old enough to make mistakes, don't step in to prevent them; let him make them. Let him not be able to roll over the first time, or crawl or walk or say the right words; let him lose a game and spill his milk and call his mother's friend the wrong name; let him not make the team and step on his dance partner's toe and get his homework wrong. And all the time still love him. Show him your mistakes when you make them, and let him see that he still loves you. Help him know that any real learning comes from mistakes, whether they are Galileo's, Newton's, Jonas Salk's or his own. While teachers grow weary of kids who have to be dragged in for extra help, I have yet to see a teacher who wasn't thrilled to spend an extra unpaid hour with a kid who asked.

17 *Don't make life too soft for your child. Let him know that learning is often hard and sometimes boring, but then so is life. As M. Scott Peck wrote in* **The Road Less Traveled,** *"Once we truly know that life is difficult—once we truly understand and accept it—then life is no longer difficult. Because once it is accepted, the fact that life is difficult no longer matters." Both life and learning are exciting and rewarding, but few of life's greatest rewards—and greatest learning experiences—come without long, hard work. If your children write these words off as parental moralizing, ask them to read about the trials of any Olympic gold medalist or Nobel scientist or to talk to a parent whose child has grown into a happy adult.*

WHY?

Children often get the idea—and I don't blame them, because teachers often give them the idea—that learning means having stuff crammed into them like supplies in a backpack. When they don't learn, then, the teacher simply hasn't done a good job of cramming. Of course, the fact is that learning is an arduous process that children must work through for themselves, and when they don't learn, chances are they haven't sweated enough. Harold Stevenson, coauthor of *The Learning Gap,* discovered that societal work attitudes resulted in a major difference between Japanese and American schooling. Since the Japanese attribute academic success to effort, their students work harder than their American counterparts, whose society attributes success to inborn ability. The lesson we can learn from the overly envied Japanese education system is that it's okay to have to try hard when learning doesn't come easily; the only blame comes from not trying.

HOW?

When your child complains to you that she is working too hard, don't do what so many parents do—complain to the teacher. Instead, tell her what a fifth-grade teacher in Morris, New Jersey, says: "Life is tough, and sometimes you have to do things you don't like."

If a child doesn't understand, help her get help; if she is sick and misses classes, help her make up the work; but if she feels put upon because she has to struggle and think and probe and research, shout, "Hurray!" and tell her that's what learning is all about. Don't take excuses. A decaying school with a poor Hispanic population on the wrong side of the tracks in El Paso, Texas, sends more students to highly competitive MIT than does any other school in the country—all because of a math teacher who makes them work. A lot of other students who are bright enough don't make it because "they have not pushed themselves," the math teacher says.

PART III
How You Can Strengthen Teaching

18 Encourage teachers to individualize their teaching.

WHY?

Students come to class programmed so differently that to try to teach them all the same thing at the same time in the same way simply doesn't work. Kids aren't learning; they know it, you know it, and their teachers know it. According to a recent UCLA study, 80 percent of college faculty felt that high school academic preparation was as poor as or worse than it had been in the 1970s, when the need for reform was clearly evident. Half the members of the freshman class these days consider their high school grades inflated, a fact corroborated by teachers, who admit to inflating grades to keep from failing half the class. So prevalent is the practice that New York State abandoned the use of high school grades as a basis for awarding scholarships, returning to the old system of using standardized tests—which, I can't resist injecting, is probably worse.

A major cause of school failure is the lack of attention paid to individual student needs. Parents and teachers alike recognize the conformity into which their children are pressed. When nonteachers were questioned in a Gallup poll about their criteria for a good teacher, 83 percent reported that they considered meeting students' individual needs either most important or very important. Teachers themselves agree: the National Foundation for the Improvement of Education reports that, of the greatest needs in schools cited by America's "exceptional teachers," almost half involved individualized instruction.

The bulk of American teachers must start realizing that they have the most heterogeneous classrooms in the world and that instead of trying to copy homogeneous Japan, they have to devise ways to reach each member of their diverse group of students. They have to deal with their different religions, abilities, interests, even languages; their different races and cultures, which instill different values and goals and expectations and customs; their different levels of achievement and maturity. In no way can they teach as they used to. When students try to learn en masse, all but a few are lost; when each student learns at his own pace in his own way, all of them can succeed. Discipline problems all but vanish with individualization, because students meet daily success instead of failure. I once watched a mixed fifth- and sixth-grade individualized class in Melrose, Colorado; so focused was their attention, so productive their interaction, that I thought I was in the presence of a specially gifted group. "Oh no," the teacher explained, "these are children who couldn't make it in other schools because of behavior problems."

HOW?

Asking a teacher to switch from a traditional class to individualized teaching is asking a great deal. Teachers have been trained to believe in traditional education and to use traditional classroom techniques, and abandoning them poses a threat. As when walking into a dark room without knowing what's there, the teacher will need to grope her way slowly in order to feel safe. Yet the change can be brought about, and has been—all across the country. Scarsdale, New York, set up an alternative junior high school when enough parents demanded it. Lagunitas School District, in west Marin County, California, created three distinct elementary school programs—open classroom, Montessori, and a more traditional academic and enrichment program—in response to parent pressure and ongoing parent involvement, resulting in programs tailored to the learning style of each student. As a principal, I have encouraged teachers who felt comfortable with more flexible classrooms to plan individualized teaching. Teachers of the first and fourth grades switched quickly, as if they had been waiting for a signal. Others followed more slowly. And some clung to the security of tradition.

You can't force a teacher into individualized teaching, so don't bombard her. Take systematic steps instead:

↰ If the school's parent group supports your interest in individualized teaching, work through that organization; if not, form your own group of parents who share your philosophy.

↰ Visit schools or classrooms where teachers have abandoned old teaching methods. Observe these teachers; talk with them; talk with their students; ask the parents how the change came about. If you can't locate an alternative school or classroom, ask your district superintendent of schools or even your state commissioner of education.

♦ Read as much as you can on individualized teaching and alternative schools, particularly books by John Holt, Jonathan Kozol, Herbert Kohl, and John Glasser. The U.S. Department of Education (Washington, D.C. 20208-56410) and your local library are good sources.

♦ When you feel comfortably prepared, make an appointment to talk with your child's teacher. But don't approach her on the attack: "What you're doing is wrong." Suggest instead that an alternative approach might work better with your child or, if other parents have joined you, with those few children. Start small. Offer her some material to read. Suggest that the principal might be interested in instituting some individualization and invite the principal to discuss your ideas with you and the teacher.

♦ When you see the principal, suggest that she invite a teacher from an alternative classroom to talk to the faculty. Ask the principal whether the district or the state curriculum coordinator might not have some materials and methods to help teachers.

♦ See if you can persuade your principal to let one or two teachers initiate individualization and then report to the faculty at the end of the semester.

♦ If you find yourself getting nowhere, make a visit to your district superintendent of schools. If you have enough parent pressure behind you, he might listen, and he, after all, is the one who can set up an alternative school within the system, as Scarsdale and west Marin County did.

With an increasing body of research indicating that individual students have their own particular ways of learning, a program called Structures of Intellect is taking hold. Tailoring curriculum and teaching style to the way each child learns best, the program has dramatically raised both standardized-test scores and student enthusiasm. Schools using their own individualized programs report similar success: Grand Rapids, Michigan, lowered its dropout rate; students in Alexandria, Virginia, found they could apply the individualized technology they learned to other subjects; Verona, Pennsylvania, was able to meet the needs of fifty handicapped and eight gifted children, along with two hundred thirty so-called average kids; I personally watched self-confidence motivate about twenty first-graders in Bloomington, Indiana, as they handled the tapes and books and hands-on materials of individualized learning. Case histories of these schools and of others in your own state will give your child's teacher the reassurance she needs in order to feel her way to the light switch in the dark room of individualization. You can locate case histories through the superintendent's office.

19 **See if you can persuade teachers to get rid of those rows of desks in the classroom and cluster desks so that students can work together in groups.**

WHY?

As a newsletter of the Coalition of Essential Schools admonished teachers, "Do not waste class time on 'teaching.'" Contradictory as this advice may sound, what the writer advocates is collaborative rather than competitive student effort. As scientists, businesspeople, and even educators gain through sharing ideas, so students multiply their learning experiences by opening their minds to other viewpoints and ideas.

I have watched groups of students in elementary, junior high, and high school working together with such absorption that they were deaf to the bell and blind to the clock; I have seen students too insecure to speak up in class become major contributors in peer groups; and I have consistently found the critiquing of essays in peer groups to be as valuable to students as, if not more valuable than, my own personal comments.

HOW?

Teachers are used to assigning students in twos or threes to special projects: it's not unusual for them to build a castle together, paint a mural, or re-create an ancient civilization; together they go with ballpoint and pad to interview a city official; and they cast a play that they have jointly written. When their collaborative projects are complete, they report to the rest of the class or perform to the applause of their proud parents, united in their effort and accomplishment.

Despite these kinds of group successes, which teachers encourage sporadically, many teachers still shy away from everyday collaborative work. One reason is that when a roomful of students work together, they break the silence demanded in a traditional class. While the quiet hum of give and take is educational music to the ears of a teacher who knows its value—an idea shared, a question posed, a problem solved, a possibility explored—to those bound by tradition, it is the sound of chaos.

You as parents should encourage teachers to try collaborative learning. Point out to them that you see your child and his friends putting in joint effort at home all the time—on assignments and chores and at play—and that there's no reason it won't work in school as well. You can get support for teachers by asking the principal to hold a faculty meeting or workshop on the value of student collaboration. However, since the most persuasive voices will be those of your children, get them to ask the teacher to let them work together on certain lessons: a difficult math principle, a history text, the novel or play they are studying. Teachers let students work in teams in science labs; why not broaden the scope? It's up to students to calm their teachers' fears through serious effort as they work together—no idle chatter, no loud noise, and no copying—and most of them succeed: teachers who let kids work together repeatedly report fewer behavior problems and a higher level of achievement.

20 *Help teachers with the endless frustration of undone homework by suggesting that they might motivate slackers and challenge achievers by setting aside traditional assignments and drawing up contracts with students instead.*

WHY?

Few teachers have not thrown up their hands in despair over undone homework and wildly creative excuses. Similarly, few parents have been spared the tortures of what I call Homework Hell—the nightly screams, excuses, tears, and pleas that arise around homework. One reason kids hate homework so much is that they consider it arbitrary: they already know it and are bored, or they can't understand it and are frustrated, or they could have done it in school if the teacher had assigned it earlier. Truth to tell, there is often little logic in the homework students are expected to spend hours on each night.

According to the U.S. Department of Education, there are more high school juniors and seniors (13 percent) who don't do their homework at all than those who take it seriously (12 percent) and spend two hours on it. Twenty-eight percent spend only five minutes to under an hour. Since over 25 percent aren't being given homework, it looks as if a large number of teachers admit to having lost the homework battle and have given up.

There is another way besides surrender, however, to spare both teachers and parents the homework agonies they suffer—and to spare students as well. The answer is to replace the same old nightly assignments that don't keep up with a child's speed or intelligence with contracts drawn up by student and teacher together for work to be covered by week's end. Contracts not only tailor assignments to each child but also enable all children to have a voice in controlling their learning—to help determine what material they feel capable of covering and to fully determine how they will allot their time in order to cover it. As partners in homework, students don't face work that is either too hard or too easy; and, by having control of their time, they can design their schedule around the TV show, the telephone call, or the social visit they really don't want to miss. Sometimes it turns out that a student is too immature to take on this kind of responsibility and reneges on the contract. In that case, she and her teacher will temporarily abandon a weekly contract and draw up one that operates on a day-to-day basis instead. As the student learns to assume responsibility, the contract can be extended to two days, three days, and finally back again to a week.

I have personally seen contracts work wonders as early as the first grade in Bloomington, Indiana; in a combined fourth, fifth, and sixth grade at the Whitby School in Greenwich, Connecticut; and in scattered junior highs and high schools across the country. Not only did children accomplish more work with less fuss, but they gained noticeably in maturity and self-confidence.

HOW?

Talk to your child's teacher about the possibility of instituting contracts. Share your understanding, and ask him to try contracts for a week and see if students don't produce better work with less tension than he sees now. If he is reluctant to try, urge the principal to discuss student-teacher assignment contracts at a faculty meeting; one principal I know of asked for volunteers to try contracts and was swamped. Remember, as always, to do your own homework thoroughly so that you know what you're talking about: visit schools, and get the opinions of teachers and students.

21 *Discuss with your child's teacher the subject of learning through discovery as an alternative to the tried-and-true "read and take notes" method of teaching.*

WHY?

When the education innovator John Dewey proposed that schools switch their focus from teaching to letting kids discover learning for themselves, he was merely echoing what wise educators from Socrates on down have espoused. As the Chinese say, if you give a hungry person a fish, he'll eat it and be hungry again the next day, but if you teach him how to fish, he'll be able to get food for the rest of his life. A good school acts as a fishing manual, giving children learning skills and showing them how to go about teaching themselves. They have to learn the letters of the alphabet in order to read, but a teacher can lead them to the adventure of unearthing the secrets of the written word for themselves. They have to memorize arithmetical rules and multiplication tables, but the teacher can help them discover for themselves why these make sense. They have to know the facts of history, but a teacher can turn them into detectives by letting them piece together historical data. They have to learn scientific principles, but a teacher can give them the thrill of finding the magic in science.

When questioned, the majority of children say they are bored with school; the curiosity with which they were born has been quashed, and their main interest becomes "Do we have to know this for the test?" Even the National Education Association, that staunch supporter of teachers, considers active student participation instead of rote learning essential to education reform. When children are equipped with basic tools and guided to the treasure trove by a teacher willing to stand back, they experience what learning is all about—the thrill of discovery. With what is called discovery teaching, Houston schools have changed middle school voices from "Science is boring—all those textbooks and vocabulary tests" into "Wow, this is my favorite class!"

HOW?

As you would with every other innovation, present discovery methods as a possibility to your child's teacher, but don't be surprised if she resists. Most teachers have been trained in having answers for children and are used to showing them how and where they will find them. Discovery learning precludes that. No longer will she have the security of being in control of her students' learning; rather, she will set the stage for them and stand aside as one of many resources. If the teacher is willing to try, however, she will reap the rewards a teacher dreams of: her students will be more involved in their work, her discipline problems will all but vanish, and what students learn will stay with them far past the next quiz.

Give teachers the support they need by urging your principal to offer the faculty a workshop; ask the district curriculum coordinator what materials are available; visit classrooms in which teachers already use discovery methods and report back to your teachers. There are many such classrooms scattered around the country. At the City and Country School in New York City, according to its director, "children's curiosity provides the curriculum . . . and teachers try not to give answers but show children how to find them on their own." At the Malcolm X School in Berkeley, California, children discover mathematics when their teacher asks the questions, but the students reason and discuss their way to the answers. In an elementary school in New York City children learn mapmaking by making their own map of the neighborhood; in a middle school in Westchester County, New York, students learn economics by operating a model city in the classroom, complete with stores and bank; in a California high school they learn the problems of the handicapped by role-playing a handicapped person for a week; and in Oregon, a sixth grade runs a bona fide book company—researching, marketing, writing, illustrating, and selling their own books as an introduction to the vast subject of economics.

22 *Let teachers know that you care less for the grades your children get than you do for the thinking they learn to do.*

WHY?

The *New York Times* reported on an apathetic fourth-grade boy turned off to school and to life. When he took an algebra class designed to make students think, it "lit a fire under him," according to his mother. "He was like a puzzle—his mind was a million pieces. She [the teacher] helped him put it together in a beautiful picture." While learning to think may not turn every child into a completed jigsaw puzzle, it certainly enhances life and leads to wise decision making.

So important does one educator consider the teaching of thinking that he instituted a program called Odyssey of the Mind to reward curiosity by making the search for answers as important as the answers themselves. Over half a million students have participated so far. In less dramatic ways schools and school systems all over the country are pushing toward the same goal—for example, the schools in Westerly, Rhode Island; Racine, Wisconsin; New Milford, Connecticut; Glenburnie, Maryland; Dobbs Ferry, New York; and Totowa, New Jersey.

Still, too many American schools cling to rote learning. A foreign student, in a letter to the *New York Times,* recently expressed her shock at the lack of critical thinking among American students compared with European students. A sign in a British school that could hardly appear in America reiterates her theme: "The teacher could be wrong. Think for yourselves."

HOW?

As a parent, you have to examine your own educational values. You know that if your child reads the text, takes notes in class, and memorizes what she sees and hears, she will get a good mark on her tests and at the end of the year. You also know, if you analyze the situation, that this kind of rote learning doesn't teach a child to reach into the many compartments of her brain and think. So what do you want: a child who learns to get a good mark, or a child who learns how to think? Of course, the two are not mutually exclusive, but since it's a lot harder to think than to take notes and memorize, your child has a better chance of bringing home an A through rote learning. However, your child has a better chance of making wise decisions and finding fulfillment if she learns to think.

When you assess your values, I think you'll come to the conclusion that thinking beats A's in the long run. So what you have to do is let the teacher know where you stand. Parents often put so much pressure on their children and on their children's teachers that thinking gives way to marks. Tell the teacher—and get your PTA or PO to back you up—that you would like to see the emphasis changed. Let the principal know what you want, and the superintendent and the board of education, too, so they can help the teacher install new methods to teach thinking.

All it takes is encouraging teachers to stop giving answers and start asking questions. At seventy-eight, Mortimer Adler, the educator who conceived of the idea of Great Books of the Western World, made the adjustment and became convinced that any teacher could do it. It means getting students to excavate what they read—to dig under the surface and figure out why and how and how else and like what and which others. It means getting them to form opinions based on facts and to weigh pros and cons. It means getting them to conceptualize and interpret and integrate and look for inference. It means turning students from receptacles filled by what they read and hear into coauthors, coinventors, and coeducators.

23 Urge teachers to assign independent study projects on a regular basis.

WHY?

According to UCLA's Cooperative Institutional Research Program, students entering college today are far less likely to have developed independent study habits than those who entered twenty-five years ago: only 10 percent do reading that is not required or study regularly in the library, and 73 percent rarely or never check out books or journals. In other words, American students learn to do what they are told but don't initiate learning on their own.

Growth is a lifelong process, with learning the chief contributor. As Gordon Allport wrote in his book *Becoming,* we never reach the peak of growth because maturity is not a goal line that we can cross in order to score and then stop for applause, but rather a continuing state of becoming. Needless to say, no one can make us become; we become on our own. If a child is not guided into the way of self-learning so that he can continue the process throughout his life, once he is out of school he will find himself at a standstill, with no one to make him learn and no skills for self-learning. Independent study prevents that standstill, for it lets kids teach themselves. It lets them grow. It lets them become.

In addition, independent study gives students an opportunity to explore areas that the school curriculum can't cover; it gives them an opportunity to open doors about which they are curious, doors that otherwise might remained closed for life. I saw a fifth-grader become an expert on Iceland through an independent study project that he chose "because I like snow" and a high school freshman fathom the symbolism of Yeats "because I saw where he lived in England."

HOW?

A good way to broach the subject with your child's teacher is to explain a special interest your child has of which she is probably unaware. It may be baseball or science fiction or surfing, all of which I have seen lead to stunning independent study projects. Urge the teacher to let your child tackle an independent study project for credit, and suggest that other kids might want to do the same. Some teachers have set aside a week or several weeks so that every student can pursue her own study; other teachers have allowed students to elect independent study in place of a particular unit of class work. I favor the former approach, since it gives all students, instead of just those who volunteer, the experience of self-learning.

In case you are wondering, the baseball project involved reading about the history of the sport and learning to calculate statistics; the science-fiction project began with analyzing the appeal of this literary form and ended with writing a story; the surfing project literally dipped into ocean currents and tides for measurements.

24 *Help teachers excite students with imaginative classroom exercises.*

WHY?

Researchers in the San Francisco Bay area recently reported, based on the results of two studies, that the more exciting and engrossing teachers can make their lessons, the more children will learn and the more they will want to learn. Since all of us can remember sitting through dull classes and lively classes, I think we knew the findings of those studies before the researchers undertook them.

Despite both the studies' results and our own prior knowledge, however, students continue to moan in unison, "School's so boring." In thousands of classrooms every day, they do their homework, bring in their answers, correct them in class, and tackle the next lesson, running like hamsters in a monotonous circle and learning just about as much. As a result, students daydream, turn off, block out, or simply sit there and yawn. Apathy, teachers agree, is a greater problem to combat and far more prevalent than disruptive behavior, a situation that California's superintendent of schools has targeted for reform. "We have to move from apathy to engagement," he says.

HOW?

It is not easy to plan exciting classes every day, every week, all year; teachers get bogged down in a curriculum top-heavy with required material, shortages of time, an overload of students, and their own exhaustion. Those who explode with creative energy often burn out, and those who just cover the material become dull. What's a teacher to do?

You might light a spark with a few suggestions to enliven the teacher as well as his students. If you can't dream up anything more stimulating than what's already anesthetizing your child, look around for other sources. The best source is the students themselves. Ask them, or suggest that the teacher ask them, to submit ideas for pepping up class work; the request in itself will send their imaginations soaring like flares through the classroom. Given a chance, children can always find ways to turn work into fun: remember Tom

Sawyer and the picket fence? I have seen students come up with ideas ranging from creating a game of Jeopardy for the study of *Romeo and Juliet* to creating an imagined fight over the Bill of Rights among our country's forefathers. An English class invented a bingo game using characters in literature instead of numbers, and I have heard of a first grade that learns numbers by playing hopscotch.

If the teacher is really bogged down, he can turn to the district curriculum coordinator for ideas. Being in contact with all the schools in the district, this person is in a position to observe a wide variety of teaching techniques and disseminate the best. Another source of help is the principal. Although you don't want to complain that the teacher is boring the children to death, you—with the PTA or PO behind you—can suggest that the whole school needs revitalizing. A faculty meeting, a workshop, a suggestion box, or visits to other schools could give the needed impetus.

Since 1952 one teacher each year has been selected as representing the best in teaching—the National Teacher of the Year. You may suggest that your parent group contact one of these teachers to see whether she or he would conduct a meeting with the faculty of your school. Following is a list of teachers who have received the award over the last twenty years; you can reach them through the schools listed after their names.

1992. Thomas Fleming. Special Education, Washtenaw Intermediate School District, Ann Arbor, Michigan.

1991. Rae Ellen McKee. Remedial Reading, Slanesville Elementary School, Slanesville, West Virginia.

1990. Janis Gabay. English, Junipero Serra High School, San Diego, California.

1989. Mary V. Bicouvaris. Government/International Relations, Bethel High School, Hampton, Virginia.

1988. Terry Weeks. Social Studies, Central Middle School, Murfreesboro, Tennessee.

1987. Donna Oliver. Biology, Hugh M. Cummings High School, Burlington, North Carolina.

1986. Guy Doud. Language Arts, Brainerd Senior High School, Brainerd, Minnesota.

1985. Therese Dozier. World History, Irmo High School, Columbia, South Carolina, now consultant to Secretary of Education Riley.

1984. Sherleen Sisney. History/Economics/Political Science, Ballard High School, Louisville, Kentucky.

1983. LeRoy E. Hay. English, Manchester High School, Manchester, Connecticut.

1982. Bruce Brombacher. Mathematics, Jones Junior High School, Upper Arlington, Ohio.

1981. Jay Sommer. Foreign Languages, New Rochelle High School, New Rochelle, New York.

1980. Beverly Bimes-Michalak. English, Hazelwood East High School, St. Louis, Missouri.

1979. Marilyn Black. Elementary Art, Bernice A. Ray School, Hanover, New Hampshire.

1978. Elaine Barbour. Sixth Grade, Coal Creek Elementary, Montrose, Colorado.

1977. Myrra L. Lee. Social Living, Helix High School, La Mesa, California.

1976. Ruby Murchison. Social Studies, Washington Drive Junior High, Fayetteville, North Carolina.

1975. Robert Heyer. Science, Johanna Junior High School, St. Paul, Minnesota.

1974. Vivian Toms. Social Studies, Lincoln High School, Yonkers, New York.

1973. John A. Ensworth. Sixth Grade, Kenwood School, Bend, Oregon.

There are too many exciting things happening in classrooms across the country to describe them all, but here's a sample:

↝ Students and staff at an intermediate school in the Bronx created GUTS—Government Understanding for Today's

Students. They surveyed their neighborhood to determine major problems and then devised solutions, some of which they actually implemented. Teachers were delighted with the students' enthusiasm—and with a dramatic rise in their reading and writing scores.

- South Pointe Elementary School in Miami teaches math by having students measure earthworms and helps poor readers by letting them write words in whipped cream.

- A high school in Pasadena teaches students about the U.S. Constitution by staging a mock trial to overturn an ordinance that led to the conviction of a white supremacist for disorderly conduct in flaunting a swastika.

- Limestone Elementary School in Sand Spring, Oklahoma, pulls art, writing, and science together by having students create brochures and plan itineraries for vacations to other planets.

- In a first grade on Long Island, children learn to read by learning to remember and reenact their own experiences, such as going to the beach, buying shoes, or riding a train.

- A history teacher in Mount Clemens, Michigan, surprises his middle school students by coming to class dressed as a historical figure and having them guess who he is.

- I have seen teachers enliven math through card games, enrich vocabulary through Scrabble, introduce poetry by having children dance to different meters, teach *Hamlet* by having students write a modern-day version, and play Name That Tune with geometry theorems instead of songs.

25 *Make sure teachers hold students accountable for their work.*

WHY?

When teachers establish requirements for children to meet and then let the kids slide by without meeting them, they are doing a great disservice to those children: they are teaching them that what they do and what happens to them as a result have no connection. Although such a lesson may seem harmless if they fail to hand in a paper or keep an appointment, it may well prove fatal if they ingest a drug or drive a car after drinking. Children who don't learn accountability for their actions go through life in a state of helplessness, believing that forces outside their control shape their destinies rather than they themselves.

It is, therefore, important that teachers hold students to the demands made upon them—and not accept the late paper (except in emergencies), not disregard the undone homework, not allow the misspellings and sentence fragments, not settle for the superficial reading. Of course, the demands have to be reachable, because if a child is incapable of meeting them, he can't be held accountable.

On the wall of her office, the principal of a Chicago school had a sign that read, "If God wanted permissiveness, he would have given the Ten Suggestions." She turned around a school in which only three of its eight hundred pupils read at their grade level by hiring teachers who would assign work that was hard, but doable with effort. What's more, she and the teachers made sure their students did it. Contrary to public opinion, stringent demands do not constitute cruel and unusual punishment—not if the demands are within a student's reach, not if teachers give the support needed to meet them, and not if failure is accepted as a step along the way. Stiff demands are a far greater kindness to children than permissiveness, which cheats them of education and allows them to grow up as victims of forces they see as beyond their control. Some of the best-loved teachers are those about whom students say, "Boy, is she tough!"

HOW?

When you tell the teacher that you want him to follow through if your child fails to do what is expected of her, be prepared for him to be amazed at first, and then grateful. He is probably far too used to hearing parents complain because he kept their kid after school or gave her extra makeup work or maybe even said she had to go to summer school. So your plea for accountability may sound strange to the teacher's ears.

Explain that you consider schoolwork your child's responsibility and that you therefore leave it up to her to do it. If she does it incorrectly, you expect the teacher to help her correct her mistakes; if she does it shoddily or not at all, you expect him to have her make up the work in any way he sees fit. With this attitude, you become a strong support system for the teacher.

In order for this system to work, though, you have to forgo the practice of rewarding your child for doing homework and punishing her for not doing it: no dollar bills for the former; no being grounded for the latter. Rewards and punishments put homework under your control, and the whole point is for your child to take control herself. When the teacher makes her stay after school or miss recess or whatever, it is not to punish her, but to ensure that she makes up the missed work in order to learn both the lesson and accountability.

26 *Let teachers know that you want your child to strive for excellence as much as they do.*

WHY?

For a number of reasons education in America has been watered down. What began as an elitist institution when it was brought from England to the young country has grown to include the most diverse population in the world. That is our nation's pride. However, in order to accommodate the large numbers of students who don't speak English, whose parents may be illiterate, whose background has not been steeped in education, and who themselves see little market value in the failing grades they get, schools have dropped many course requirements and have lowered standards. The fact that national test scores have fallen below those of many less industrialized nations indicates not that our students are less intelligent, but that we are not teaching them to their potential. The National Education Act's first principle for education reform, resoundingly echoed by teachers, states: "Mastery of what is taught must be America's standard of educational excellence."

A debate has raged in the United States through the years since John Dewey first proposed a new approach to education, which the public tagged "progressive education." What he wanted was child-centered learning, with individualization, discovery, and a collaborative rather than competitive classroom; what he got was misunderstanding and misuse that turned classrooms into chaos and permissiveness. The debate still rages: traditional versus progressive education, excellence versus laissez-faire—the either-or mind-set that has retarded educational reform ever since.

Parents, teachers, students—please realize that standards of excellence can be maintained in both kinds of education as long as educators demand them. Every level of learning has its own standards, and what teachers must do is set them at a challenging but reachable level and see that children meet them. I advocate individualization, since it lets students reach for excellence at their own levels of capability on their way to the top. The teacher who demands that all students rise to the same level simultaneously dooms a percentage of her class to failure in school; but the teacher who lets students slide by when they don't meet the standard dooms them to failure in life.

Students need to strive for excellence. They can. Their teachers will show them how. The chairman of RJR Nabisco summed it up this way: "To turn our public schools around we need to adopt that legendary Noah principle: no more prizes for predicting rain; prizes only for building arks."

HOW?

Don't undermine a teacher when your child complains that the work is too hard; after all, no one promised him a rose garden. Check the assignments to determine whether the goal the teacher has set for him is attainable—not easily, but with hard work. If you think it isn't, you, your child, and the teacher should sit down together and talk in order to understand the relationship between your child's learning level and the assignments. If, however, you think the work is challenging but doable, the three of you ought to have a talk anyway to reinforce the child's self-confidence in tackling it.

On the other hand, if the child grumbles that school is "too easy . . . kid stuff . . . last year's rehash," take just as careful a look. If you feel that the teacher is demanding too little of his students, tell him so. Don't confront him accusingly, but let him know that you expect more of your child and that you want him to expect more, too. If the problem lies not with a single teacher but with the school as a whole, the PTA or PO should firmly let the principal know how the parents feel. If he can't—or won't—take steps to raise the school's standards, you and the parent group will have to seek action through the superintendent or the board of education.

It can be done. The population of Cardinal Ritter School in St. Louis refuses to let standards fall despite some troubled low achievers the school admits. A *Readers' Digest* article highlighted the experience of one student who entered this school with a negative attitude and a 1.7 grade point average. Although threatening to quit after a year because "all we do is schoolwork," he stayed, buckled down, and graduated with a 3.8 grade point average and a college scholarship. What changed him? Teachers who "chastised me when I needed it, who encouraged me when I was down, who I knew I could always depend on."

27 *Help teachers get to know the kids in their class as people, not just as students.*

WHY?

In a survey students at all grade levels were asked what single quality they considered most important in a teacher. The answer was overwhelmingly "Someone who cares about us." Yet we have all had teachers who obviously cared more for the so-called pearls of wisdom that dropped from their lips than for the students with whom they interacted five days a week. Today, more than ever before, students come to school carrying burdens that far outweigh the problems on their math assignment or the dates facing them on a history test. Ninety percent of teachers are aware that alcoholism, abuse, and neglect are problems their students face. Since parents, often either absent or nonexistent, tend to be the source of the problem, who is left to help troubled children but teachers?

"Remember, the children who come to your class are not born anew each day on the doorstep," a principal I know told his faculty every September for years, and a teacher in the National Education Association echoes his words today: "We must get people to realize that today's kids are facing things that we couldn't have dreamed of fifteen or twenty years ago."

It is essential that teachers relate to their students as people, not as marks in their grade book, in order for them to teach at all, because children who feel depersonalized simply can't learn. When treated like robots, they act like robots, going through the motions with no commitment. As the psychologist Jerome Bruner, who developed learning concepts, says, "When schools show they care, the students respond with better behavior and higher achievement."

So desperate are young people for supportive contact with an adult and so unavailable is it in many homes and schools that a California psychologist devised a way to provide it through technology. By dialing one of ninety-four numbers, students can hear prerecorded messages covering alcoholism, sex, eating disorders, homework, compulsive gambling, date rape, and suicide. Through their own medium, the telephone, young people get advice and hear a warm voice.

Other schools offer still warmer voices in the form of
teachers who consider themselves counselors and friends as
well. In Intermediate School 70 in New York City, for
instance, teachers are actually paid an extra stipend to serve
as mentors, meeting small groups of students for breakfast
and planning shared activities in the afternoon and evening.
Since the program began, truancy has dropped dramatically,
homework assignments are handed in, and achievement levels have soared above national averages. In most schools,
however, teachers take on the mentoring role simply because
they care, which is exactly what the teachers at Ned O'Gorman's famous Children's Storefront in Harlem have been
doing for twenty-five years. Starting as a preschool offering
an oasis amid the city's horror and now continuing through
ninth grade, the school considers caring to be basic to learning and living. As Ned O'Gorman says, "It all comes down to
love."

HOW?

Some teachers never lose the feeling of the child they once
were; others have to learn to remember. I have known teachers who feared that if they let their guard down, students
would lose respect for them, and I've known teachers who
honestly thought that only minds were housed behind the
faces that looked at them each day. Since teachers rise to the
level you expect of them, according to Jerome Bruner, you as
parents are in a good position to let teachers know where
that expectation level lies.

Talk to your child's teachers about his human needs. Let
them know that he and the other children in the class have a
stack of worries and hurts and insecurities that often stand
in the way of their schoolwork. If teachers are hesitant, suggest that the children be encouraged to do some writing
about their feelings or talk in small groups or even, as I have
seen, make tape recordings. Some teachers have helped students communicate at this level through music or role-playing. Painting is one of the most successful mediums for the
expression of feelings. In the seventies, a third-grade teacher
in Brooklyn asked her class to draw what they were afraid
of; among the big black blobs and monster faces were the
guns and bullets of the Vietnam War. A teacher can initiate a

discussion of feelings through academic study by simply having students relate what they are currently reading to their own lives, for instance.

Many schools assign a faculty adviser to each student so that no child will be deprived of an empathetic ear. However, since student personalities and the degree of empathy among faculty ears differ, it sometimes works better to have students select their own advisers. The point is that you, the principal, and the students assure teachers that you consider the human touch basic to growth and learning. But you have to believe it yourself first.

28 *Encourage teachers to downplay grades.*

WHY?

A survey in public, private, and parochial schools found that over three-quarters of students admit to cheating, primarily on tests or homework. Students in academic trouble tend to cheat by copying a friend's homework, since they either are too undisciplined to do it themselves or truly can't do it. However, top students, it has been found, cheat far more—on tests and other assignments by which they are evaluated. So focused are many achievers on marks that although they know they can pass any test or write any report and receive a high grade, they so fear pulling down a B instead of an A that they won't take a chance. As head of a school, I experienced this firsthand when the highest-ranking senior plagiarized two term papers with the excuse "I didn't want to disappoint my teachers."

Cheating is only one reason to de-emphasize grades; equally important is the distorted competition they create. Whether stamped in red on a paper or posted on the bulletin board, marks evoke an eternal cry—not "What did I learn?"; not even "What did you learn?"; but "Wha ja get?" which translates into "I hope your mark was lower than mine."

You have to teach kids competition early, parents say; get them ready for the real world. Perhaps the parents' world is as real as they claim because *they* were taught competition early. In other worlds, such as that of the Zuni or the Inuit or that of the kibbutz, where children are not marked against each other and taught to compete, kids grow up to prize cooperation instead. It can work in America, too: in a series of studies, Adelphi University proved the strength of collaborative effort; and 65 percent of the educators at the University of Minnesota who analyzed grades over a period of fifty-six years found that cooperation promotes higher achievement than does competition. Spiro Agnew fell far short of fact when he predicted that if America eliminated the competitive drive, we would become "a waveless sea of nonachievers." Even the most ardent ethnologists and animal behaviorists admit that the cooperative drive existed alongside—and probably before—the competitive drive.

Schools that focus on the whole child rather than limiting their goals to his academic growth alone tend to de-emphasize grades in favor of more accurate and inclusive kinds of evaluations—comments that draw a portrait of a student's attitude, effort, and strengths as well as his achievement. The principal of Indianapolis's Key School sums up why: "We eliminated grades and encourage children to cooperate so that they can help each other, learn from each other, and not feel that they don't want to try because others can outperform them in an area."

HOW?

Most parents were schooled in a system that awarded marks for achievement, receiving rewards for A's and B's, frowns for C's, and maybe actual punishment for D's and F's. And let's face it: a mark by any other name, be it Excellent or Needs Improvement, smells like an A or an F to a child. As a result, parents do unto their children what was done unto them: they, too, use marks as the final evaluation of worth. Some go so far as to pay for A's and B's. But then, schools pay, too—with gold stars and honor rolls. A professor at the University of California wants even the government to pay: he suggests that Washington administer the Scholastic Aptitude Test and pay students in the top 5 percent fifteen thousand dollars each and those in the second 5 percent seventy-five hundred dollars each.

That is the kind of thinking you as parents can quash. Begin with your own family, refocusing educational goals from getting good marks to learning. Let your children know that learning always entails hard work and often entails mistakes along the way as well—mistakes that are made not from not trying, but from undertaking challenges, exploring new areas, and taking risks. With this attitude, children see failure without the stigma otherwise attached to it, accepting it as a step toward learning. Anyone who achieves anything worthwhile is bound to fail along the way. Thomas Edison, whose many inventions we accept as a routine part of life today, met with lots of failures for every success. Did Alexander Graham Bell get his phone to ring on the first try? Did Jonas Salk end polio with his first experiment? Did Isaac Newton wait until the apple hit him to try to explain gravity? No way.

When you and your family trust your new attitude, let the teachers know how you feel. It's not easy for them to abandon marks or even to put less emphasis on them, as I discovered when I ran a school. For even though your family may have seen the light, many students will feel that the pins have been knocked out from under them. Conditioned to decide how much they have learned and how well they have learned it by the marks they get, they have no other means of evaluating themselves. And without marks on a report card to guide them, their parents, even more discombobulated, have no easy basis for praise or punishment.

So go easy on the teacher, who stands on the firing line. Support her efforts to downplay marks by getting the parent group behind her; a good speaker can spur parents on. The office of your state education commissioner probably has material on alternative marking systems, and there may even be schools nearby that have already instituted less competitive ways to evaluate students. Most Friends, Montessori, and alternative schools have given up traditional marking. Check them out. While your child's teacher is in a position to de-emphasize grades in the classroom, it will take the principal or the district superintendent to abandon traditional grades altogether.

29 *If you can't get rid of grades or the emphasis on them, suggest that teachers evaluate students on a more just and meaningful basis than the results of tests.*

WHY?

A new report from the National Association of Secondary School Principals states that students should be evaluated on their ability to probe, to integrate what they learn, and to present it, and that this should be done in a way that has greater educational value than the mark they get. "Most common tests probably fail on all three counts," adds the coauthor of the report.

Educators design tests for the so-called average student, who doesn't exist, according to Howard Gardner's school research group Harvard Project Zero. *Average* implies a single framework, yet since Gardner identifies at least seven kinds of intelligence—linguistic, mathematical, spatial, kinesthetic, musical, interpersonal, and intrapersonal—teachers should evaluate students based on many different frameworks. Every child, the Harvard group asserts, has at least one outstanding strength among the seven kinds of intelligence and one relative weakness, with varying combinations of all seven; the tests to which children are subjected week after week and upon which their whole future often rests take no account of about three-quarters of their intelligence. If a child's strength lies in linguistic or mathematical intelligence, he gets into Harvard; if it lies elsewhere, he may still not get into Rhode Island School of Design or Juilliard unless his teacher and his school have broadened their evaluative methods enough to recognize his strengths.

Furthermore, when children receive marks based on test results, the tester has to assume that the results are typical of that child's work and ability. Yet studies indicate that test results often vary by as much as 50 percent, depending on how the child feels, what kind of stress he is under, and what happened to him the day or the hour prior to the test. And let's not forget the possibility of error among teachers: I have seen the same essay test receive an A from one teacher and a D from another.

It is important that students know how they are doing in school—what they have achieved and in what areas they need further help—but unless an evaluation assesses the full measure of a child's development, it means little.

HOW?

Many schools have given up standardized tests, other than those required by law, and even at the highest level change is taking place. For best results, however, change should start in the classroom and spread through the school by word of the teacher's success with new methods of evaluation.

Talk to your child's teacher about innovative ways to measure student learning. Vermont and Connecticut use what are called portfolio evaluations—the results of long-term student projects—which, unlike tests, let a teacher build on what a child can do rather than on what he can't. New York's commissioner of education may also have his state's schools give them a try.

Many schools determine marks through conferences in which the teacher and student together assess the student's effort, progress, strengths, and weaknesses and together determine the grade he deserves. To the surprise of teachers, a good many students tend to underrate rather than overrate themselves, although the majority come up with the same rating their teachers do. To the surprise of parents, such children have few complaints at report-card time, saying, "I'll do better next term" more often than "The teacher's not fair."

Some schools avoid marks by evaluating students with a simple pass or fail, accompanied by a detailed comment slip. Others skip the pass-fail step and rely on lengthy comments from each teacher instead. Feeling that tests and marks are both inadequate and destructive, I have throughout my professional life experimented with alternative systems of evaluation. Although well-thought-out comment slips are more time-consuming for teachers, they give both parents and students far more specific help. Since they enable students to feel good about what they have accomplished and to zero in on what they still need to do, in the long run they help teachers, too.

Even comments, however, become meaningless unless they are composed with understanding. A second-grade teacher at a school where I taught wrote, "Molly can't read because she is immature." When the headmaster saw the comment, he demanded that the teacher show more insight, writing back, "If you can't be immature in second grade, when can you?"

Contact schools in your district or state that have instituted alternative testing systems; the district superintendent of schools or the state commissioner of education can direct you if there are such schools. You might also seek information from schools that are outstanding in testing reform— for example, J. Graham Brown School in Louisville, Kentucky; Joel Barlow High School in West Redding, Connecticut; New Market Middle School in New Market, Maryland; and Sullivan High School in Chicago.

30 See whether the teacher will let the students evaluate her at the end of the year.

WHY?

The only kind of evaluation most elementary- and secondary-school teachers receive is one in which the principal or an assistant principal sits in on their class and then either sends them an evaluation form or—if they are lucky—has a ten-minute chat with them. Usually the principal alerts the teacher a day or so ahead of his proposed visit; the teacher then alerts the students; and as a result, the class period is tense and unnatural. Kids are wonderful; they rise to the occasion, loyal to the poor teacher under scrutiny, and act like the little angels she never sees the rest of the year—no spitballs, no fresh remarks, no talking to neighbors, not even any yawns.

While the teacher is grateful to be let off the hook, she really doesn't learn much from such an evaluation. The principal may point out how well she times her class work or how sound her lesson plan was, but he doesn't know—and she doesn't, either—how well she really teaches. Does she communicate clearly? Does she sustain energy? Is she enthusiastic about her subject? Has she a sense of humor? Does she care about her students? Is she flexible? Is she well prepared? Does she know her subject in depth? Is she willing to give extra time and help?

No one is in a better position to judge the effectiveness of a teacher than her pupils. While the ratings are not always complimentary, they are shockingly honest: of twenty-two thousand top-ranking students surveyed, over 50 percent said they have had as many as three unqualified teachers; 37 percent said they have had up to ten. Student evaluations let students do something about this situation.

When they are asked to evaluate a teacher, students tend to tell the truth as they see it, and a teacher can easily spot the few who use the opportunity to get even for a bad mark or a scolding. They can spot those trying for brownie points, too. Benefits accrue to both sides: students feel they really matter when a teacher turns to them for an assessment of her teaching; the teacher, on the other hand, receives firsthand advice that no one else is in a position to give her. In my years of teaching I have picked up assorted pointers in this way that I never learned in school—from not laughing at my own jokes to letting students spend more time rewriting their essays.

HOW?

Suggest to your child's teachers—or ask the president of your parent group to suggest to all the teachers at a faculty meeting—that they try the idea of student evaluations. Although they may be somewhat frightened at first, chances are that once they muster enough courage to put their egos on the line, they will be glad they did. Students should not sign their names to the evaluations, and no one should review the comments but the teacher herself. To assure anonymity, one teacher I know insists that students write their comments at home on a typewriter or word processor, but I have never found this necessary.

In order to get kids to write specific comments, teachers should not ask the obvious "What do you think of my teaching?" The question is too vague and tends to elicit replies like "It's O.K." or "It stinks." I have found that by asking two specific questions, I get answers I can really digest: "What do you think was good about this course?" and "What do you think I should change?"

31 *Get teachers to take advantage of the teaching aides they have in abundance—other students. The subdued noise of students helping each other is certainly more productive than the ominous silence of not learning.*

WHY?

When children skip into their kindergarten class each morning, they naturally run to the play areas they most enjoy, with the friends with whom they play best. Billy learns from Jane how to build a house; Jane learns from Billy how to line up wagons. One helps the other. Anyone who has observed small children at play can't help being delighted at their generous advice giving: "No, you do it this way!"

In most first grades, however, Billy and Jane stop teaching each other how and start listening to the teacher. When they make mistakes or don't understand, they raise a hand, waiting quietly for the teacher to come and explain. Almost from the start, the teacher has too many waving hands to tend to and complains to the principal, "I need more help."

The truth is, the teacher does need more help, but what he may be unaware of is that it is close at hand. Across the country schools are calling upon the expertise of children to help each other and, in so doing, to help the teacher answer individual needs he can't handle alone or even with the limited help of an aide. Given their flexibility, alternative schools find it easy to team up a third-grader who is good in math with a first-grader who can't add, or a third-grader who has mastered phonics with a confused first-grader. Even traditional schools can fit a child's free periods into sessions for giving and getting extra help.

No one balks when older children help younger ones. Junior high students tutor in elementary classes in many schools, such as those in Montgomery, Alabama, where a peer tutorial program called Project Bootstrap has been developed. It is not unusual for high schools to give a credit point to students who serve as teacher aides on a regular basis. What many teachers ignore, however, is the fact that students within their own classes are just as well equipped as older students to offer help. A fourth-grader reading at the seventh-grade level or a sixth-grader who has mastered fractions is as capable of helping a classmate as an older child.

Students helping students produce one of the rare no-lose situations in education: the teacher gets the aides he needs; the students receiving help are able to learn; and the student helpers grow in self-esteem. It's there. It's free. And it works.

HOW?

Parents can take two routes to help establish student aides in the classroom. One way is through the principal. If your child is having trouble with a subject, suggest that the principal ask a proficient student to tutor him; if your child happens to be the proficient one, ask the principal whether it wouldn't lighten a teacher's load to let your child serve as a tutor. Not having thought of the idea herself, she may be somewhat jolted at first, but the possibility of having a way to calm that harassed classroom teacher might quickly take shape in her mind as a blessing.

The second route is through the teacher himself. If your child is having academic trouble, point out that another child might be able to help him out of it. Let the teacher know that you understand he hasn't the time to give extra help to each child, and suggest that pupils could help each other. From my first year of teaching I have called on student help—in recollection, I think, of the help I got from a classmate when I cried because I couldn't do long division.

32 *Go in to meet your child's teachers at the beginning of the year, while the slate is still clean and no problems have arisen. Express your support of the school and your eagerness to be involved.*

WHY?

Most schools schedule an open house sometime during October, a time for parents to meet the teacher, sit in the classroom, and be alerted to the year's plans and programs. Although every parent's children have been going to school for six weeks by that time, and have been tackling the programs described, creating images of themselves for the teacher and their peers, and stowing away the teacher's images of them, parents have not been included. Furthermore, although open house is a time to give the teacher a brief hello, it is not the time to discuss your individual child or your desire to participate. At open house you look and listen; you don't speak.

Speaking waits until the first time your child comes home crying that he failed the test or complaining that he has too much homework or screaming, "I hate my teacher!" Then, like Raging Bull, you charge into school, angry and defensive, to confront the teacher. The teacher, who has struggled to learn her pupils' names, lost sleep correcting papers, and fought to get the audiovisual equipment to work, faces you angry and defensive, too. What a start to a partnership! Not only can't you get to know each other; you can't even solve the problem that got you into the ring in the first place.

Teachers are human, and with a confrontational introduction like that, it's as hard for them to erase the first impression as it is for you. Try as you may to counteract it, that teacher will always retain for you a touch of Godzilla, just as you will always retain for her the threat of Medusa. An elementary-school teacher I know always tells her parents at open house, "We promise to forget what we hear about you in the faculty lounge if you'll forget what you hear about us at home." It's a good idea, but memory isn't always that malleable.

A lot of long-term hostility can be avoided if parents and teachers meet early in the year, before problems arise. That means a week or two after school opens, when children are on their best behavior and teachers, still reviewing, haven't yet hit them with hard work. An unemotional parent-teacher introduction offers the promise of mutual support and of shared hopes and efforts for your child.

HOW?

At the end of the first week of school, ask the teacher whether you may stop by for a few minutes the following week; or if you are picking your child up at school and see the teacher off duty—and I mean *not* supervising sports or loading the school bus or talking with another teacher—ask whether he has a few free minutes.

Since the purpose of meeting with him this soon is merely to introduce yourself and express general support, don't attempt to do more than that. You can cover several points quickly:

- Let him know that education is important to you and your family.

- Assure him that you want to help in every way possible.

- Make it clear that although you will help your child, you want your child to assume responsibility for learning.

- Ask him to please let you know if a problem arises so that you, your child, and the teacher can solve it together.

So productive is an early parent-teacher meeting that many parents and teachers encourage it in a more formal way. Some teachers send a note home inviting parents to stop by before school opens; others prefer to meet parents before or after hours after school opens. Class mothers and fathers have been successful in planning small coffee hours in their homes or at the school, to which they invite parents and the teacher. If neither the teacher nor the class mother or father in your child's school initiates an early meeting, you should suggest it to one of them.

33 *Urge teachers to set up weekly communication lines with parents.*

WHY?

Three-quarters of the problems that arise in schools, according to administrators, come about through a breakdown in communication: children, parents, and teachers wait till an explosion to talk to each other and don't listen to each other when they do get together. As a result, only the bad news circulates, and only when it's too late for straight talk and honest listening.

Studies report that teachers who keep lines of communication open between the classroom and the home have fewer problem children and problem parents than those who don't. So why aren't more teachers making the effort? Time. Teachers are so overburdened with too many students, too many extra duties, and too much paperwork that the thought of additional notes or phone calls home might be the last straw. There are, however, ways around this problem.

HOW?

Many teachers are keeping in close touch with parents without either shortchanging their students or overextending themselves. What they do is let their students become the communicators. In practicing various ways to send word from their classrooms into their homes, students learn how to gather information, how to discriminate in selecting newsworthy material, how to organize their thoughts, and how to write coherently and accurately—essential skills they will use for the rest of their lives.

One of the most successful techniques for encouraging such communication is for a class to develop an informal weekly newspaper, which students type or write on a word processor, duplicate, and deliver in person to parents every Friday afternoon. Students rotate responsibility for the newspaper's content, which may include coverage of classroom activities, an interview with an interesting member of the school population, a human-interest story, an editorial about a current school issue, and perhaps a puzzle.

One school gets rid of the overabundance of its classroom

animal life—most recently, nine baby mice and an elongating python—through ads in the class newspaper. Ads that request needed supplies have brought in everything from toilet paper to typewriters, sewing machines to stilts, along with the ABCs of art books, bikes, and crutches.

Another teacher uses the class newspaper to help make difficult decisions by including a questionnaire for the parents to fill out and return. For instance, do they think the upcoming overnight trip should be (1) a camping trip; (2) a visit to a historic site; or (3) an experience in a big city? In this way, class members can view their parents' opinions alongside their own and reach a joint decision.

Modern technology has solved the problem of communicating for some schools. The Center for Parenthood Education at Vanderbilt University has set up a system of telephone answering machines to link the school and the home in several Alabama schools and in Atlanta, Georgia. At one end, parents can call the school at any time to hear the teacher's daily message about homework assignments, class work, or upcoming exams and can leave a message of their own. At the other end, the teacher can program the school's computer to call parents in the evening, when they are likely to be home, with important reminders. Although installation is costly, the system saves money in the long run, since the district must pay about three thousand dollars to rehabilitate every student who fails, according to the principal of one of the Alabama schools.

At the other extreme of modern science is the third-grade teacher in Newton, Massachusetts, who—believe it or not—sends home to every child's parent at the end of each week a page-long handwritten letter. "She's new and wonderful," a father told me. "We just pray she doesn't burn out."

34 *Appoint a class mother and/or father who will actively support both the teacher and the parents.*

WHY?

Effective class mothers and fathers serve as aides to make the teaching team—parents and teacher—work best for students. While they may handle chores such as lining up cookie bakers for a class party or building a stage for a play, they have more important roles.

On one hand they can address problems that may be developing in the classroom, such as a teacher's loss of control, by talking with the teacher, and with the principal if necessary. Sometimes their responsibilities turn out to be more serious: it was a class mother in a New York suburb who alerted the principal to sex abuse; another who verified the fact that a teacher had hit a child's head against a wall; and another who discovered a teacher with a drinking problem.

On the other hand, the class parent can quell rumor and gossip among parents as she hears it go in one ear and out many mouths in whispers and phone calls. She can go to the source, ascertain the facts, and call a meeting of class parents. If the rumors prove to be true, she can sound a call to action; if it turns out they are false, she can call a halt. A few years ago, a class parent in Florida saved the job of a history teacher accused of being un-American because he included the study of communism in his course on comparative governments; and every day across the country class mothers and fathers are in a position to stop rumors of teachers' incompetence and gossip about their personal lives.

What even the most active of class mothers and fathers seem to forget is that they are a conduit not only for bad news, but for good news as well. Spreading the word of something wonderful that's happening in the classroom can often drown out a dissatisfied hum.

HOW?

The first step a class mother or father should take in order to use the job to its full extent is to become aware of that full extent. Don't think gofer; think chief of staff. The second step is to keep in close touch with the teacher throughout the year, because she is your primary source of news. Don't worry about contacting parents; you'll be the first to know what's on their minds.

As soon as you take on the role of class parent, make an appointment to discuss your function with the teacher. Even if he expects no more than the usual chaperone-brownie-and-dunking-booth help from you, he will, overworked as he probably is, be grateful to learn that you are offering more. However, when you explain the full extent to which you plan to take on the job, he may shy away as he would from a KGB agent. Therefore, explain your job as one of cooperating with him to make a strong year of teaching and learning.

- Ask him to let you know of any problem he runs into. If it stems from him—loss of class control, for instance—you and he can discuss it and find a solution; if it stems from the outside—rumor, for instance, or an administrative directive—you can handle it at the source.

- Assure him that you will alert him to any problem you see or hear about as soon as it develops, not letting it grow beyond manageability. You will work for a solution with him or with whatever created the problem on the outside.

- Let him know that the good things going on in his class-room are important to the parents of the class and to the whole school, maybe even to the community at large. Ask him to call you or send home a note about exciting projects the kids are doing, unusual trips they are taking, and speakers they are inviting, and ask him to let you visit the class once in a while to see for yourself. Then promise to follow up by sharing the excitement—sending a flier home to parents, telling the principal, or, if there's a really newsworthy story, alerting the local media.

If the class parent presents this kind of support and encouragement at the start of the year, the teacher will welcome her, trust her, and gladly enlist her for his team.

35 *At some time during the year, plan a social get-together with the teacher, students, and parents.*

WHY?

Too often parents forget that teachers aren't there to chastise their children but to help them learn; too often teachers forget that parents aren't there to thwart their efforts but to reinforce them; and almost all the time students forget why they are there at all. The hope, then, is that teachers, parents, and students will join hands from time to time to remind themselves that they are playing on the same side in the same game.

One way for a teacher to reinforce class unity is to bring her students and their parents together with her for a social activity. Put the business of school aside and let it be sheer fun—no lectures on the goals of education, no rap sessions on student-teacher relationships, no pleas for parent participation—just fun. Psychologists tell us that group play is a bonding experience, and anyone who has ever played baseball or been part of a theater presentation or gone on a Scout camping trip understands what they mean.

HOW?

Toward the middle of the year, suggest a social get-together to the teacher. You might point out that although all of you are linked by the same classroom, the same teacher, and the same hope to get your kids educated, you all work as separate units—*work* being the key word; you don't really know each other as people. A party of some kind would bring you all together as friends.

As you know, and certainly as the teacher knows, she has no time to be a social director. Therefore, assure her that if she and her students decide what kind of activity they want, you parents will plan and execute it. Classes have undertaken minor activities like getting together for coffee and dessert as well as more adventurous ones like going on a picnic, a hike, or a trip to the beach. One class I know of decided on an overnight camping trip at a nearby site that provided six- to eight-person tents. The kids provided sleeping bags and all-night conversation; the parents provided hot dogs, marshmallows, corn flakes, and the need for sleep; the teacher provided the chewing gum she forbade in class and gratitude for her own pup tent. They did it only once but talked about it till the class split up at graduation.

36 *Urge your child's teacher to let the children know that mistakes are signs not of doom but of learning.*

WHY?

American children opt out of doing an assignment more because they are afraid of getting it wrong than because they don't want to; they have learned through painful ego smashing that doing something "wrong" in American schools means "You're a failure," and they've been hurt too much to keep trying. Although such defensive behavior may protect what remains of their self-esteem, it builds a block to learning.

Learning by its very nature entails risk—the risk of falling down when a toddler tries to walk, the risk of looking clumsy when an adolescent learns to dance, the risk of missing the ball when an adult learns tennis. School from day one involves children taking risks—the risk of not understanding, the risk of letting their parents down, the risk of not pleasing the teacher—risks about which they have no choice and with which they often have less than a fifty-fifty chance of coming out on top. It takes the courage of a soldier to face that every day for twelve years, which explains what a high school dropout once told me: "I just got battle weary."

People who can depend on support when they fail in their risk taking will keep on daring to stick their neck out—if mother comforts the toddler with assurances, if the dance partner smiles and suggests starting over, if the tennis opponent admits it was a tough shot and says you'll learn. Confident that they are okay human beings, accepted and even loved, students can shrug a shoulder and accept mistakes with the inevitability of death and taxes. Embarrassment is in the eye of the beholder.

Most schools seem unaware of the defeatism with which they enshroud error. When a student risks presenting an assignment or an answer in class and gets it wrong, he feels branded with the public humiliation of Hester's scarlet *A*. Though the dunce cap is gone from the teacher's desk, her finger of shame continues to point at the luckless child who falls short. In his book *Shame: The Exposed Self,* Michael

Lewis explains that shame is a strong force in establishing a child's behavior in relation to achievement as well as to his intra- and interpersonal life. The worse a child feels about himself, the less able he is to learn, the more mistakes he will make, and the worse he will feel about himself—a vicious circle, which he can break by copping out. If he doesn't try anymore, he won't have an ego problem because the decision to fail will be his, not his teacher's.

Urge your child's teacher to be like the Scarsdale, New York, history teacher who shouts joyously at a student's mistake, "That's a great wrong answer!" Urge him to think of error as an arrow pointing to what still needs to be done. Just the other day I told one of my students who had written a helter-skelter essay with no unity, "Thank heavens! Now we can zoom in on the problem." They do not want, nor do I want them, to continue writing disunified essays; they know that, but they also know, as I do, that with the stigma gone, their self-esteem intact, and the mistakes corrected, they will tackle the next paper with greater confidence and, probably, with unity.

HOW?

Let the teacher know that you think the mistakes your child makes should be regarded as positive steps toward learning and should not, therefore, carry a negative connotation. Caught up in a school system that nourishes itself only on success, however, the teacher may need a great deal of encouragement from you.

- Give him a copy of Harold W. Stevenson and James Stigler's book *The Learning Gap* to read.

- Talk with him about the teacher in the Midwest who challenges her students to solve a problem, be it in math, science, or everyday living, that is beyond their learning level. If they give up, they get no mark; if they try half-heartedly, they get a B; if they really stick their neck out, they get an A. Whether they solve the problem correctly or not is irrelevant.

- Suggest that he write detailed comments on student papers that support and reassure students when they make mistakes.

⮲ Urge him to send a letter home to parents asking them to encourage their children to risk new experiences even at the cost of making mistakes.

⮲ Ask the teacher to talk to parents at open house about keeping their child's mistakes in perspective. By reaching them early in the fall, he may prevent a whole year of damage.

Make it clear to the teacher that in urging him to encourage children to risk error, you still expect him to maintain standards of excellence. You don't want him to make a choice between supporting error and striving for excellence; they are not mutually exclusive, and you want both. You can have both when student goals are set high but student feet are allowed to stumble in their climb to reach the heights.

37 *It would improve education tremendously if all teachers understood child development. Unfortunately, that's daydreaming, but see what you can do to turn the dream into reality.*

WHY?

Developmental psychologists tell us that a child grows through consecutive stages and that if she bogs down at one of them, she can't skip it and move on to higher levels. There she will remain arrested into adulthood and for the rest of her life unless someone is able to help her go back and master that stage. That done, she can continue the healthy, consecutive climb. Jean Piaget showed us the stages of mental development; Lawrence Kohlberg and Carol Gilligan, those of moral development; and Erik Erikson and Abraham Maslow, those of personal development.

Yet, despite its importance to the entire learning process, most schools of education put too little emphasis on the process of child development. For instance, classrooms across the country abound with children with low self-esteem—minority children who have absorbed prejudice, abused children who see their own inadequacies as just cause for their abuse, neglected children who feel unworthy of care, overprotected children who've been given no opportunity to build self-confidence, children who feel stupid or ugly or unloved. Yet self-esteem, we hear repeatedly, is the basis of learning: unless a child believes he can, he can't . . . and usually won't. Isn't it essential that a teacher know the stages through which a child grows to attain self-esteem? Isn't it essential that a teacher know how to help him master those stages?

We know from Jean Piaget that there are four periods of mental development: up until age two, the senses develop; from two until seven, language and drawing; from seven until eleven, concrete operations like problem solving and the organization of knowledge; from eleven to fifteen, formal operations dealing with abstracts and future reasoning. If a junior high student hasn't learned to use his problem-solving abilities, there is no way he can deal with abstracts; if a third-grader still lacks language skills, there's no point in giving him problems to solve. Teachers have to understand normal mental development in order to help children along the way without pushing them into failure and frustration, and in order to guide those children who are unable to follow the normal route.

Lawrence Kohlberg devised a theory that explains children's behavior in terms of levels of moral development. Early on, children learn to do what is "right" because mommy and daddy say so; later, because they are afraid of being punished if they don't; later still, because their peers set the rules . . . and so on until they assimilate their own personal code of morality. Unless teachers are aware of the developmental steps of moral understanding, they can't possibly deal with a child's behavior. I have seen teachers punish a child for "not acting like a good citizen" at a time when good citizenship was not a moral imperative the child could comprehend because he was at the developmental level dominated by the moral code of his peer group. An effort to help the child see the negative results of his behavior might not only have a better chance of reaching him, but might also enable him to climb higher on the moral ladder.

Erik Erikson explained personal development using the term *identity crisis,* a developmental stage at which, in normal progression, an adolescent becomes aware of himself as a distinct unity. He reaches this stage only after attaining and growing beyond rising levels of identification in childhood—with parents, friends, and a broader circle of adults. Abraham Maslow also explained personal development as a series of stages at which certain needs arose and were fulfilled. A child begins with the physiological needs for food and drink; when those are met, he seeks fulfillment of needs for safety—security, freedom from fear, a sense of law and order. So a person grows through succeeding stages of need for love and esteem until he reaches the need for what Maslow calls self-actualization, the state of being all a person is capable of. A teacher unaware of the developmental progression of personal growth can hold a child back from his potential. She can block the all-important identifications with peers and with herself, and she can leave the needs for safety, love, and esteem unfilled, like gaping chasms.

Only when a teacher learns what to expect of her students—of their intellectual, moral, and personal growth—at various stages can she reach them where they are. Through success, she will minimize her frustration, and through understanding, she will heal the wounds of children snagged on a rung of the developmental ladder. You may be able to help your child's teacher reach such understanding.

HOW?

When you get to know the teacher, bring up the subject of child development. Make her aware of your concern that the school not push children, either academically or personally, beyond their limits. Since many parents, as you know, not only want the school to push but do a lot of pushing themselves, tell the teacher that you hope she will guide your child into growing at his own pace. If he seems bogged down at some point and needs extra help, you hope she will let you know. Otherwise, you want him to have a happy school experience that will enable him to learn and grow in all dimensions of his personality.

The psychologist Eda LeShan wrote, "Fun is when you feel challenged to do your best, when somebody needs you, and when you are proud of what you are doing." Teachers who respect the developmental needs of their students can make going to school that kind of fun.

A friend of mine broached the subject of child development to the teacher of one of her children, who ended up so convinced of its importance that she persuaded the principal to bring a speaker on the subject to a special faculty meeting. You may be that lucky; if not, go to the principal yourself. You alone, or the parent group as a body, may volunteer to arrange, or suggest that the school arrange, for a child-development specialist from the school district, county, state, or local community to speak to faculty and parents on developmental basics and their implications.

The teaching innovations suggested in this section of the book are being used in different ways by many schools around the country. While they have run into some resistance from traditionalist parents and teachers, they have succeeded in turning students on in exciting new kinds of schools. With students suddenly eager to learn, no longer bored, and too engrossed to complain, tradition is giving way to innovation, and innovation to learning.

The middle and high schools in Croton-on-Hudson, New York, provide one example of this educational rebirth, which they call *active learning*. In this case, the change was brought about through the Coalition of Essential Schools, a group formed in response to Brown professor Theodore Sizer's proposed education reforms. You can get specifics on reforming your school from this group. After studying the material, you may want to join the coalition. You can contact it at the following address:

Coalition of Essential Schools
Brown University
P.O. Box 1969
Providence, RI 02912

PART IV
How You Can Strengthen Administration

38 *Urge the principal to define the school's goals.*

WHY?

A definition of school goals may seem superfluous in the face of the overflow of printed materials on the subject available from state and national departments of education, but the truth is that these publications are often written with rose-colored ink. Although a dream team of educators may define goals for their schools—honing kids' basic skills, giving them a body of information, building their study habits, stretching their minds, awakening their creativity, developing their social awareness—there is often little indication of such goals in the classrooms. The functional goal in most cases turns out to be getting kids into the next grade. Handing in assignments, answering questions in the back of the book, taking notes in class, passing pop quizzes based on those notes, studying for exams, passing for the year, and moving ahead to second grade or junior high or high school or college—that's what successful teachers expect from successful students, and that's what successful principals point to with pride. In an interview, the author, educator, and vocal advocate of reform Theodore Sizer said that the status quo is what administrators want as long as their students are able to rack up prestigious college admissions. "Their only criterion," he adds, "is getting kids into college."

However, schools can be more than assembly lines along which students pass until they become finished products, because learning has an intrinsic value at each level of education. The goal of schools should be to aim for that value and help kids develop, without resorting to big talk and educational jargon to disguise their ineptitude. Yet according to the National Assessment of Educational Progress, goals are so inadequately defined that parents and teachers can't even agree on what they are: a majority of parents consider moral standards the chief goal, while a majority of teachers call lifetime learning the real aim of education. No one can shoot straight arrows when the bull's-eye is invisible.

Clearly administrators have to tackle the subject of school goals and come up with a clear definition that will unify the whole school population and set students on a course of learning.

HOW?

It's not easy. I served on a committee of representatives of about twenty education organizations that met once a month for three years, and, despite my urging, we never got around to addressing school goals. Instead we came up with tests and marking systems with which administrators felt comfortable, and we had a lot of fun exchanging anecdotes. But we never tried to answer the most important question of all: what are we trying to accomplish?

You can be more successful, though, since you have two points of strength our committee didn't have: your child, and the other school parents and their children. Make your concern an issue for the whole parent group. Send an ad hoc goals committee to the principal with an approach like the following: "You know, we look around and see the school function on a day-to-day basis, but we can't see where our children are heading. Maybe you can straighten us out. What actually are the school's goals?"

If the principal begins to reply in broad and all-too-familiar educational jargon, ask her to speak instead in specifics that will enable you and the other parents to have a clearer picture of the school's program. If, on the other hand, she is specific and defines goals in concrete terms of marks and test scores and college admissions, you have to make it clear that you want more for your children than competitive scores. When administrators who want to look good on paper (read: national test scores) pass the word to teachers that they have to produce high scores or else, teaching becomes focused on the wrong goal, and learning isn't focused at all.

Let me illustrate with a story about a school that defined one of its goals as stimulating students' curiosity through scientific investigation. The school's science teacher in fact did just the opposite by abandoning labs and fieldwork and substituting weeks of memorizing the Latin names of plant and animal species. When the bored students asked why they had done this, the teacher replied, "Who knows? They might be on the SATs." Parent pressure finally forced out the biology teacher, who defended himself with the excuse that the principal had told him not to turn the kids into scientists but to get them into college.

Scandals have arisen in many areas of the country when teachers were discovered going to the length of cheating in order to look good and to make sure the school and its students showed up well in national ratings. Some of them changed what students had marked on answer sheets, and others, more ingenious, secured the tests ahead of time and gave students the answers. While many principals were as outraged as the public, some, it was discovered, had actually participated in the fraud. The victims, of course, were the students, drilled like robots to achieve what the school considered a priority instead of being given the chance to experience what learning is all about.

Ask the principal of your school—and get the parent group behind you on this—to put together a committee of parents, teachers, students, and administrators to probe into the subject of goals. It will take time, and a lot of brainstorming and talk and research, but if you are determined, you will emerge with a firm understanding of where the school is headed and what part each one of you will play in getting it there.

39 *The next step is making the principal design the school on the foundation you've erected.*

WHY?

Change does not come easily, and administrators have a handful of reasons to avoid it, not the least of which is money. The underlying reason, however, is fear: change threatens a school with loss of control. While the faculty or curriculum or administration may be far from effective, at least people are familiar with them and, having so far survived even minimally, feel in control. Only when life becomes unbearable are they willing to risk change. On a global scale, in the eighties we witnessed eruptions stemming from unbearable conditions in Communist nations when the people felt they could no longer endure oppression; on a national scale, in the sixties we lived through change when students across the country followed in the steps of their protesting Berkeley counterparts because they could no longer endure having no say in their education and in society at large. And today schools tremble from the earthquakelike rumblings of parent pressure, student failure, teacher anger, and their own hopelessness. "Carpe diem" was the desperate cry in Cincinnati, which undertook a dramatic restructuring of its floundering school system and, according to its superintendent of schools, met with none of the usual resistance, since people felt that the system having hit rock bottom, any change would be an improvement.

Change is in the air and on the airwaves in the mouths of politicians and pundits, but if it is to involve more than the customary Band-Aids, it has to address issues. Abraham Maslow suggested destroying the entire school system and starting from scratch. I doubt whether he meant it, but he made a point. An administrator can heed his point by taking a long look at the goals his school has defined and coming up with changes to meet them.

Not all change, of course, means improvement. When a principal institutes new methods on the basis of what is good for him rather than for students, change can lead to disaster. In New Jersy, for instance, principal Joe Clark locked the fire exits to prevent kids from cutting classes and expelled droves of misbehavers from school in order to maintain discipline. Despite the sudden fame that accrued to him over his "cleanup," he was sued and left the school. A temporary principal steamrolled somewhat similar auto-cratic changes in a Brooklyn school, which a teacher described by saying, "He has brought hell to the school."

The changes a principal brings about have to stem from the educational goals the school has defined. Obviously, they have to be within the law, have to meet state requirements, have to be practicable, and have to be, if not endorsed at first, at least understood by everyone in the school. Some states have found the need for change to be so profound and the system so entrenched that instead of redesigning exist-ing schools, they have reformed by developing alternative schools. California, New York, and Washington together have 40 percent of the nation's alternative schools, with Michigan, Illinois, Oregon, Florida, and Texas offering many as well. Kentucky, on the other hand, is trying a broader approach by turning its entire education system into what the *Wall Street Journal* called "a giant laboratory for school reform."

Most schools, however, can incorporate new attitudes and methods into their current modus operandi. This has been done successfully in many of the traditional boys' boarding schools, where no one would have expected the status quo to bend. It has also been done in public schools everywhere. I did it myself in a school I ran. How?

Some years ago I gave a speech at a conference of princi-pals that I titled, "There's More to Running a School Than Meets the I." Successful change has to come from the bot-tom up. I know, because a good deal of the material in my speech came from mistakes I had made in trying to effect change from the top down.

After your school circulates its newly defined goals, urge the principal to draw up a list of changes he would like to bring about in order to meet the goals. As head of the school, he has an overview that other segments of the school population lack and is, therefore, in the best position to draw up blueprints for a new program. As a matter of fact, recent studies report as conclusively as studies can that the most important factor in raising the standards of a school is the quality of the principal. However, he can't do it alone:

- He should ask teachers, parents, and students (some schools have even involved the outside community) to select three or four representatives to form committees with him.

- These committees, with input from their full constituency, should draw up changes they think the school needs in order to meet the new goals.

- The principal should then meet separately with each of the committees to review their suggestions alongside his own and be open to argument, explanations, insistence, and compromise.

- After the principal and each individual committee have reached an agreement, all the committees should meet with him to draw up a composite picture. In suggested areas of change where all members either agree or disagree, there will be only smiles. However, in areas where teachers, parents, and students stand adamantly opposed, the principal will have to make some authoritarian decisions. He is, after all, where the buck stops; and if he can't live with a desired change, he will have to veto it.

- Finally, the changes as decided upon will be presented to the entire teacher, parent, and student body with assurances of support and the promise of hope.

40 Try to convince the principal to develop a more flexible teaching system.

WHY?

Most schools function by the bell, which signifies the start and the stop of forty- or fifty-minute periods. In an attempt to synchronize their lessons with the bell, teachers often have to leave students with unanswered questions, cut short their comments, and eliminate material of their own that would bring depth and enrichment to the class. In describing a child's ten most traumatic fears, developmental psychologist Erik Erikson listed the fear of interruption as one of the greatest, yet the school system is built on interruption. Just the other day I heard an English teacher tell a class, after looking at the all-ruling clock, "I'm sorry, we won't have time for you to finish your story. Maybe tomorrow." Words such as hers resound to classroom ticktocks throughout the country.

Not only are students cut short day after day; they are also compartmentalized. Between the ringing start and stop of one set of bells, they concentrate on English; along comes another set, and they concentrate on math; then come science, and French, and history, and art, and music, and gym. There is no carryover: as students walk from one class to another, they drop one mind-set and take up a new one to see them through the next forty minutes. At rare moments, a miracle occurs that lights a teacher's day: a student suddenly realizes, "Oh, that's like what we learned in history!" Alas, moments like these come too seldom.

Integrated learning usually happens by chance, not by design. The system reminds me of an antique desk we had when I was a kid, with six cubbyholes at the back. I see students as they walk from class to class arranging themselves, like notepaper, envelopes, stamps, and receipts, in first one cubbyhole and then another. The young mind can't turn off so abruptly. It can't refocus so suddenly. Why should it have to?

Learning doesn't occur in self-contained boxes or between the ringing of bells, like punches in a prizefight; it comes from all directions, at any time the mind is open. Even though educators know this, too many of them adhere to a rigid schedule that "keeps the wheels rolling," as they say—

the wheels of bureaucracy, perhaps, but not the wheels of learning. Some educators, however, are finding ways to eliminate compartmentalized teaching and standard-length class sessions by developing a more flexible schedule. Urge your principal to try to do the same. The Cincinnati schools, for instance, are experimenting with two-hour class periods.

HOW?

Schools can integrate the teaching of subjects in a variety of ways:

- Team teaching in most schools brings two or three teachers together to plan a course that covers related subjects such as literature, art, and music. However, a school in New York has found a way to integrate math, reading, science, and social studies by using the kitchen as a lab. The program is called "Kitchen Science," and it allows kids to study measurements (math), digestion (biology), ethnic foods (social studies), and following recipes (reading).

- Some years ago, a New Jersey school created a system of teaching by total immersion (the Berlitz School approach to language teaching), which has been tried by other schools. The New Jersey school divided the year into five or six segments, each one devoted to an individual subject area, so that when for example French was the focus, students studied the French language, French history, French literature, and French art and music. Although science and math had to stand on their own, teachers brought in contributions from France to whatever extent they were able.

- Teaching by theme rather than by subject immersion has had greater success. This practice allows schools to take a general theme—the hero, for instance, or the search for self—and tie to it those subjects that lend themselves to it, such as English, history or social studies, and the arts. Just recently New York's chancellor of schools has proposed creating schools that focus on broader themes such as world trade and the environment.

- It is also possible to teach by historical period. The school may devote a semester to the study of the eighteenth century, for example, using materials dealing with that period to teach English, history, the arts, and perhaps even science.

While only the most nontraditional schools have been able to fully adopt any of these systems, many schools have shaped parts of them to fit their own needs: the Worcester Elementary School in Massachusetts ties subjects together; the Hemingway School in Idaho integrates computer classes into the traditional curriculum; the schools in Derby, Kansas, coordinate nutrition education with the breakfast program; Sir Francis Drake High School in San Anselmo, California, offers the option of a one-semester integrated-studies program in which all subjects focus on a single theme; Cambridge, Massachusetts, pulls teachers together to integrate reading, writing, and drawing instruction; and the high school in Charleston, West Virginia, has restructured its entire curriculum to accommodate interdisciplinary teaching.

Schools have also found ways to loosen up their rigid schedules:

~ The most bizarre innovation was the six-day week, which some schools tried early on. This system took as day six Monday of the second week, Tuesday of the third week, Wednesday of the fourth week, and so on. Although it proved to be too confusing for most schools, it did drive home the point that scheduling changes were imperative.

~ Some schools give each teacher a double period once or twice a week so they have time for class workshops and lessons in greater depth.

~ Some schools add an additional period at the end of the day to make time for programs that could not otherwise be scheduled.

~ Other schools lengthen each class period from the usual fifty minutes to an hour and schedule classes four instead of five times a week. This eases up the schedule while keeping the total amount of time students spend in each class the same.

~ Schools that use team teaching double the time allotted to each two-teacher class without having to redesign the schedule.

Schools that have initiated varied changes such as these to integrate teaching and loosen the schedule have at least one thing in common: the changes haven't cost them an extra cent.

41 *Even when money is short, don't let the administration cut arts programs.*

WHY?

When a Gallup poll asked people what courses they thought should be required of non-college-bound public-school students, art and music were at the very bottom of the list. In the national plan called America 2000, in which a recipe for ideal schools was formulated, the arts were omitted from the core subjects entirely, even though, in conjunction with the National Endowment for the Arts, the U.S. Department of Education did issue a pamphlet admitting that "all students can benefit from appropriate arts instruction." In schools all over the country, as funds dwindle, administrators do not hesitate to hack away at arts programs. While no exact figure exists, it is estimated that in over half of our schools students have no instruction in art and music, and in even fewer schools are dance and drama offered. Much of the general public and many administrators feel that such classes are mere frills and do not prepare students to get a job, and that, further, they take money away from courses that do. Stick to the basics, they say. "Arts education in the public schools is very much at risk of being eliminated if we are not more vigilant," warns Carol Sterling of the American Council on the Arts.

Yet what is more basic than the arts, humankind's first means of expression? Art has appeared on cave walls in France, in African drumbeats, on the stages of ancient Greece. What is more basic than the arts to the history of civilization? Though they blossomed in the Renaissance, the arts have had to fight the stifling exploitation of tyrants throughout the years.

The arts program in a school is not intended to teach children to become painters or dancers any more than the science program is intended to teach them to become botanists or biologists. It fosters creativity and self-esteem; it extends their capacity for enjoyment and assures them there is more to life than academics; specifically, in the no-nonsense words of the Council for Basic Education, "it can enhance the basic curriculum by teaching students to observe, to reason, to study, to read (in the broadest sense), to speak, to listen, to compute, and to write." Marilyn Polin of Cutler Ridge Middle School south of Miami provides living proof: many of the students in the arts program she created have dramatically raised their grades in other subjects.

The kindergarten through eighth grade art teacher in Sherman, Connecticut, recently wrote to the local paper pleading with the community to vote down budget cuts that would have pared away a large share of the arts program. "I am the Sherman Art Teacher [her capital letters]," it began. "I feel disarmed, if you will, by not being given the opportunity to explain the scope of my program before it was cut. I feel further disabled in that none of you has observed Art in action in Sherman." Maybe that's why parents and principals rush to cut the arts when monies are low: they haven't seen them in action.

The arts are vital to the full growth of all children, but particularly so to those in academic trouble or emotional turmoil, whose only success may come from a creative endeavor. Cut off from any realm of achievement, these children compound their failures; but when they find success in a picture they paint or a tune they play, their raised self-esteem spills over to success in other areas as well. The arts give children a unique opportunity to express themselves with fun and freedom while school rules and demands in other areas constrict them. In addition, through singing, dance, and drama—not to mention those extravagant murals and collages that classes collaborate on—children learn the value and the joy of cooperative accomplishment in what is usually a far-too-competitive environment.

So vital to learning do some educators consider the arts that they have developed schools with a major art focus. Four years ago eight Indianapolis teachers asked themselves, "Why shouldn't someone who is good at art be told that this is a wonderful strength?" Their answer came when they created the Key School, a public elementary school that gives children an opportunity to grow in all the areas of intelligence posited by Harvard University's Howard Gardner in his Project Zero. In the South Bronx, St. Augustine School, a K–12 school that was about to close because of low achievement and underenrollment, went even further, transforming itself into a school specializing in the arts.

Today it is one of only three schools in New York City where 98 percent of the students meet state academic standards.

The Nashville Center for the Arts, a southern version of Lincoln Center funded in large part by Leonard Bernstein's estate, extends the arts throughout Tennessee in a series of summer workshops where teachers learn to incorporate drama, music, and dance in their regular classroom teaching. So committed is the center to learning through the arts that it is currently developing an arts-centered curriculum in one school as a pilot program, with the hope of further expansion. Other states such as Florida, South Carolina, Oklahoma, Minnesota, and New York have also taken innovative steps to keep arts education alive and well.

HOW?

As a parent who believes in the value of art as both enrichment and learning, you can exert the educational power bestowed on you through your tax money and your children to keep the arts in your school. First, arm yourself with facts: read all you can on the arts in education; write to the National Arts Education Center at New York University, 26 Washington Place, New York, NY 10003. Ask your state education department to send you materials.

Next, embark on a campaign to convince everyone involved that the arts must stay strong in your school. Begin by rousing the parent group: copy materials for them to read; ask the Art Teacher (yes, capital letters) to speak to them; bring in an outside speaker, a local artist perhaps or a prominent businessperson who shares your cause; get parents to visit arts classes.

Now argue your case before the principal, the superintendent, and the board of education. Finally, alert the outside community to the imminent danger threatening the school's arts program. Distribute fliers, and hold an open house to which everyone is invited and at which they can hear speakers and ask questions.

If, despite your efforts, the administration votes out the arts program, you still have a way to keep it around. If your community is no different from most, it has painters, sculptors, potters, musicians, actors, and dancers—not all professional perhaps, but committed to their creative fields. They have doubtless been aware of your campaign and supported it; now they are in a position to offer real help. Make an effort to enlist several of them as volunteers to keep the arts alive in your school by teaching a class once or twice a week. Although you can't pay them, you can promise them a better school for their community and a population growing in support of the arts they love. Approach local museums and theaters, and music and dance groups in your area; perhaps they will donate staff time. Check their performance programs to identify the companies, organizations, and individuals that support them financially, and try to sell these supporters of the arts on the idea of helping your school maintain an arts program as well.

42 *If your school is large, urge the administration to break it into smaller units—schools within a school.*

WHY?

History shows that people act differently as part of a mass than they do as individuals. After the 1992 Los Angeles riots, shocked participants admitted that they hadn't intended to vandalize and loot but "just got carried away." On the other coast, police found that some members of a crowd of teenage boys "wilding" in New York's Central Park were as appalled as their parents and neighbors at their participation in mob violence that was nearly fatal. And veterans of the Vietnam War still suffer trauma over the brutal acts they would have resisted under normal circumstance but willingly became a party to as whole platoons ravaged villages and human beings.

In the same way, students lose their identity in the mass of a large school. While they may not rape and murder, as nonpersons they don't feel known, cared about, or responsible to anyone for their behavior. As a result, large schools see greater vandalism, a higher dropout rate, and lower achievement; when students feel they are unimportant to their teachers, they also feel unimportant to themselves. My college students prove this to me every year. Despite the general complaint—and the admission by students themselves—that they cut classes and don't do homework assignments, I get regular attendance and honestly done homework. Why? Because I have classes of only about twenty students—as opposed to lecture classes of hundreds—and I am therefore able to give them a great deal of extra help and attention.

As educators see evidence that large schools either don't work at all or work far less successfully than they should, some have made changes.

HOW?

The easiest way to break a large school into smaller units is to develop schools within a school. A high school I know of in suburban Westchester County, New York, divided itself into four "houses," each having a faculty head and a quarter of the school's population; house assignments were determined by lottery. The house was the focal point from which the students' personal and social lives emanated, with the result that the students, lost in the crowd before, began to develop a sense of belonging: teachers and peers knew each of them as individuals, and they as individuals felt a sense of responsibility to their house that they hadn't felt toward the more impersonal school.

New York's former chancellor of schools Joseph Fernandez devised a different way of building schools within a school. He suggested assigning different classes to different floors, where they would share teachers and counselors, or assigning students in different disciplines to different floors—for example, math and science to one floor, athletics to another, the humanities to a third. He created the program in thirty-two high schools—primarily to reduce the dropout rate, for he was aware that with a greater personal touch, students gain incentives both to stay and to apply themselves more energetically.

Many cities develop magnet schools to break large high schools into smaller units. Each one specializes in a particular discipline—business, science, languages, law, medicine, and so on. Each magnet school draws students according to their area of interest. Unlike New York's Fiorello H. Laguardia High School of Performing Arts and the Bronx High School of Science, to which students gain admission on a competitive basis, magnet schools, like regular high schools, accept all who apply. New York City at this time has 133 magnet schools. Philadelphia, on the other hand, has instituted a citywide program in its twenty-two high schools that creates a kind of family for students, clustering two hundred to four hundred students together with eight teachers who stay with them from ninth through twelfth grade. "You create small, intimate communities and young people have something to attach to," an education professor at the University of Pennsylvania explains.

If your child is in a large school, you—with the parent group behind you, as always—should talk to the principal about the need to form small groups within the school. Suggest ways this can be done with little disruption, point out the benefits, and give her a few examples. If she feels powerless to effect such a change, take your cause to the district superintendent, who has greater authority and may be in a better position to follow through on the change you propose. While the establishing of magnet schools may have to emanate from the office of the state education commissioner, dividing a large ongoing school into smaller units can be done at the district level. You'll need strong support from parents, teachers, and students; you'll also need convincing arguments. Contact the schools mentioned earlier that have gone this route to find out how they went about developing schools within schools and what results they have seen.

43 Urge the principal to set up ongoing professional development programs for teachers.

WHY?

Surely everyone can remember teachers (and we're lucky if it's only a handful) who resurrected the same old notes, pulled out the same old examples, drew the same old pictures on the chalkboard, and made a stab at humor with the same old jokes, which our older siblings and parents said weren't even funny the first time. We sat through those classes bored and turned off to learning. I heard a sixteen-year veteran of teaching brag once that she had taught sixteen classes over the years; I knew that, on the contrary, she had taught only one class for sixteen years. Her last fifteen classes undoubtedly knew it too.

Teachers need to keep abreast of what's new in the world: new literature, scientific discoveries, national and international events, new heroes and villains. They can do that in part by reading newspapers and magazines. But more is needed. Teachers need to be aware of the constantly new educational materials being created, of the latest research findings on child development and learning, of new teaching approaches to motivation and creativity. They need to hear from other teachers, to share their experimentation and successes and failures.

Teachers know what they need, and they want it. In a recent poll commissioned by Apple Computer, Inc., and the National Foundation for the Improvement of Education, when asked what they considered essential to reaching national education goals, three-quarters of the teacher sample said more professional development for teachers. The National Education Association itself in its fight for school improvement listed "meaningful professional and staff development programs" among its top priorities.

As a teacher at Rye Country Day School in Rye, New York, I did not spend a single year of my eleven years there without attending at least one teacher workshop or conference in addition to talks and discussions within the school. During two summers I took courses at the University of Maryland—all of these with the blessing and financial outlay of the school. Nor was I alone in my continuing professional development: most of the faculty followed a similar pattern. As a result, we knew what we were doing in the classroom, did it well, and had fun doing it—the fun that comes from new challenges and the self-confidence to meet them.

HOW?

In the days when schools could afford to send teachers to a university program at night or in the summer, classrooms came alive. And not just those teachers' classrooms, but other classrooms throughout the school as new ideas and renewed enthusiasm recharged the whole faculty. Whatever the school spent was paid back tenfold in more exciting teaching and more excited learning.

Alas, today few schools can afford such expensive renewal, so administrators have to either shortchange their faculty or devise new ways to attain renewal. You as a parent and the entire parent group can play a large part in assuring teachers of continued professional development. Here are a few suggestions you can offer the principal:

- The principal can provide workshops at zero cost by having any of his own outstanding teachers conduct them.

- He can send one teacher to a course or a workshop for which he must pay and then have that teacher convey what she learned to the rest of the faculty. (In many schools, parents raise the money to pay for that one teacher's tuition.)

- He can invite workshop leaders from other schools that have programs he wants to develop.

- He can locate appropriate workshop leaders through the superintendent's office.

- He can inform his faculty of grants available through the National Foundation for the Improvement of Education (1201 Sixteenth St., N.W., Washington, DC 20036), many of which are used for professional development. Through foundation grants, Delano, California, was able to bring together seventy-seven teachers to learn new techniques for teaching writing; Gainesville, Georgia, provided teachers with release time to develop a dropout-prevention program; Lexington, Kentucky, helped teachers use telecommunications; Campton, New Hampshire, helped teachers design a new science program; Glouster, New Jersey, gave in-service training in math; and Sanford, North Carolina, taught teachers how to counsel students on sex abuse and domestic violence.

The PTA or PO in your school also can raise money, as many parent groups have done, to pay the cost of a workshop or a university course for a worthy teacher.

44 Ask the principal to set aside days for teachers to visit other schools.

WHY?

Teachers have told me that they get more new ideas from watching other teachers teach than they do from all the courses they took in college. This makes sense, since the flesh and blood of a class in progress is real life, and real life is what teachers face every day—the questions, the arguments, the deaf ears, the daydreams, and, when they're lucky, the boiling excitement. Observing one teacher vault a hurdle where another is stuck or catching on to one teacher's solution to another's insoluble problem can breathe new life into a dying teacher and resurrect an already-dead class.

HOW?

Suggest that your principal phone principals of other schools to request that several of his teachers be allowed to visit. He should be specific—stating, for instance, that the visit would include kindergarten, third-grade, and fourth-grade teachers or ninth-grade English and advanced-placement biology teachers—so that the teachers can be steered to the best in the host school. That school's principal will alert his teachers to expect the visit on a given day. An offer of reciprocal visits at your school is in order.

Your principal will learn a lot if, after the visit, he has a short meeting with each teacher to keep abreast of what she saw and heard—especially what new ideas she picked up. If these seem really innovative and applicable to your school, the principal may ask the teacher to share them with the whole faculty. I know an English teacher who through a visit to another school got the idea of playing charades in class, using books and characters the class had studied; she found it a successful way to review because the kids had fun. She passed it on to the history teacher, who used it, too.

Principals tell me that although they think teacher visits are a great idea, they can't afford substitutes to replace the teachers for the half day they're gone. However, some schools have found a way around the lack of funds: they use parent volunteers in the classroom during the visit, sometimes assisted by a student aide. Other schools simply call a holiday, letting the whole faculty set up visiting appointments on the same day; they get no complaints from the students.

45 *Ask the principal to let teachers visit each other's classes within the school.*

WHY?

The principal knows as well as you and the students which are his best teachers and, unfortunately, which are his worst. Some teachers may be bad because they have simply been around too long and, being tenured, can't be replaced; others, perhaps inexperienced, may just need strong support and new approaches. Those who are worn out the principal has to either live with or move from the classroom into an area where they can't do so much harm; principals have salvaged classes by "graduating" teachers into the administrative office or into the position of audiovisual specialist and then finding a challenging classroom replacement. However, a principal can actually save insecure teachers by letting them observe top teachers in action. New teachers or those giving such an abundance of energy that they teeter on the brink of burnout are in a particularly good position to gain and regain vitality and know-how from star members of the faculty.

HOW?

The most effective way to set a teacher-to-teacher plan in motion is for the principal to suggest the idea at a faculty meeting and then leave it up to the teachers themselves to follow up informally. When I taught in Rye, New York, the other teachers and I were in and out of each other's classrooms during free periods throughout the year. I still remember watching a teacher open a hidebound classroom by circulating among the desks as he helped each student individually in rewriting an essay; the technique helped me then and still helps me today with my college students. In observing the class of a fellow faculty member whom you really admire, a glorious moment comes when you discover that he does something the same way you do; it's like writing a phrase that you later find in Hemingway or Faulkner.

46 *Try to set up a mentor system within the school.*

WHY?

As reported in the *New York Times,* Professor Fuhr of Clemson University uses the term *marginal* to describe the bottom rung of teachers, those who just get by. Although not incompetent enough to qualify on union terms for firing, they overlook homework, maintain poor discipline, retreat from new approaches, and stick to timeworn material that leaves their captive audience of students turned off. Because they have tenure, the principal can't replace them, and they haven't done anything so blatantly horrible that the union will agree that they should go, so they continue on year after year, in great part responsible for undone assignments, unlearned lessons, cut classes, and dropouts.

Professor Fuhr cites three kinds of marginal teachers: those who are new and poorly trained; those who have personal problems; and those whose lack of self-control leads to verbal and sometimes physical abuse. Hair-raising as it sounds, schools subject your children to unfit teachers every day and then punish your children, not the teachers, for not working and for acting out their frustration.

Some schools, however, have realized that the fault frequently lies not with the student but with the teacher and have taken steps to eliminate marginal teachers. One way, as was pointed out earlier, is to transfer them to areas where they won't have to deal with students; another is to move them to another school, where they can start again with a new attitude and a clean slate. The most common way, however, is to assign a mentor to them.

A mentor is one of the experienced, successful teachers whom every parent wants his child to have, every student loves, and every principal wishes he could clone. When a new teacher joins the faculty, the principal assigns a mentor to her, who in mother-hen fashion familiarizes her with school personnel and procedures, saving her from the first weeks' confusion that comes with the job. As soon as the new teacher feels comfortably at home, however, the mentor takes up the more important role of teacher's teacher: he observes her class, giving support and suggestions; has her visit his class; and throughout the year keeps a close eye on her as his special charge.

In Rochester, New York, after making a one-year evaluation of a new teacher, a mentor has the responsibility of recommending that she be either retained or let go. With new teachers thus carefully screened, schools find themselves stuck with fewer tenured marginal teachers later on. If, however, a marginal teacher slips through to tenure or a good one loses her effectiveness, the principal can assign a mentor to her as well for counseling; in extreme cases, he can put her in a retraining program. If after receiving all the help a school can provide, a teacher continues to be unable to do the job, the kindest thing a principal can do is tell her she is not cut out for teaching. With dread I did this once, only to receive a sigh of relief and a big "Thank you."

HOW?

Ask a group of parents to join you in talking to the principal about the mentor system. Be as specific as you can in pointing out the new teachers who suffered through their first year because there was no one to help them correct and redirect their teaching and who could have spared themselves and their students much pain if mentors had been at their side. Also point out that there are currently some dreary teachers in the school who should have been weeded out at the beginning. He'll know who they are, because he hears the voices of parents each year pleading to have their children transferred. In a kind of Russian roulette, however, he has to assign a few classes to these teachers despite his misgivings. When you talk to the principal, don't hedge; bring up names. If he tells you his hands are tied, suggest that he untie them with the mentor system.

With the mentor system in place, the entire school will benefit:

⌁ Students will have better teachers.

⌁ Because of better teachers, parents will have more positive attitudes toward the school.

⌁ Teachers will have greater self-esteem. At present 69 percent of them agree that their faculty needs upgrading.

⌁ The principal, no longer feeling guilty and harassed, will justifiably take more pride in having the buck stop at his desk.

47 *Ask the principal to let teachers evaluate each* other.

WHY?

Traditionally principals have visited teachers in their classrooms, usually by appointment, but sometimes on a drop-in
basis. Based on one or two of such visits, the principal
writes an evaluation (or, worse still, fills out a form), which
he shares with the teacher in a short interview. I have sat
through enough of these interviews to know how little they
improved my teaching. What I usually heard from the principal was, "Looked good. Keep it up." Although I felt my job
was secure, I wanted more feedback about my teaching.

When a principal observes and evaluates a teacher, she
poses a threat, no matter how great her tact, because she is,
after all, the head coach who hires and fires the other
coaches. When teachers evaluate one another, on the other
hand, they act as teammates on an equal footing. With
greater firsthand knowledge, they can offer each other specific criticisms to strengthen weak points and reinforce what
already works; similarly, since such evaluations don't carry
the threat of job loss, teachers don't have to put up resistance but can take their peers' suggestions right into the
next class.

HOW?

It is important that teachers' evaluations of each other be
kept confidential. The principal is not to see them, nor are
other teachers, since their success depends on mutuality: I
tell you what I see, and you tell me. Period. Their sole purpose is to enable teachers to grow professionally, not to
determine who is good enough to be a mentor and who is
bad enough to be fired. I have never seen them not work out;
on the contrary, I have seen them break down barriers
between teachers, changing them from competitors into col-
leagues.

You might get such peer evaluations going in your school
by suggesting the idea to the principal or to a group of
teachers. At St. Augustine School in New York City teachers
follow up observations of each other by pointing out one

thing the teacher did that they would *not* do, and why; and suggesting three things they *would* do, and how. A pre-scribed formula like this might make the original plunge easier for teachers; once they have taken it, they are bound to like the waters.

48 *Carry the idea a step further and urge the principal to let teachers evaluate themselves.*

WHY?

Since a principal is required to enter an evaluative report in each teacher's file during the course of a year, she can't just let teachers evaluate each other and call it a day; eventually she has to look at them herself as the Boss. However, she doesn't have to follow the traditional authoritarian path but can use a more democratic method, which also happens to be more effective.

Schools have found that when teachers are asked to evaluate themselves, they are incredibly honest in sizing up their weaknesses. One teacher sees that he takes too long to correct papers; another that his assignments are unimaginative; still another that he tends to lose his temper. While some teachers are too modest to list their assets as accurately as their liabilities, most welcome the chance. Those who have elicited comments from students find a wealth of material to include. In being part of the evaluative process, teachers can't cling to the old gripe that since the principal doesn't see them on a daily basis, she can't know how good they are. If the teacher himself knows how good—and how bad—he is and evaluates himself accordingly, he has to consider the evaluation fair.

HOW?

Obviously, the principal can't file away the teacher's self-appraisal as the year's formal evaluation, but she can merge it with her own observations. The principal should invite the teacher into her office to discuss the self-evaluation. Agreeing on some points, disagreeing on others, the two will come up with a composite evaluation far more accurate than the one the principal would have written herself. The principal will be relieved to share the burden, and the teacher will be free of resentment.

49 Now comes the principal's moment of truth: ask her to let the faculty write evaluations of her.

WHY?

Since studies show that a school is only as good as its principal, you want to get the best principal you can. And no one knows how good a principal is better than the teachers who work under her direction. They are the ones she may burden with paperwork, tie up in an inflexible schedule, or force to pressure students for high scores; she may water down their curriculum, or pick at details and miss the meat of their teaching. She is the one who may side with parents every time they complain, keep her office door closed to teachers, and never learn the names of students. On the other hand, the principal may be the one who sets goals in which teachers believe, supports them in their efforts to reach these goals, adheres to excellence, and values each student as an individual. Most likely, she is a combination of both aspects.

From reading teacher comments, a principal will gain the kind of insights the poet Robert Burns had in mind when he wrote about the power "to see ourselves as others see us." Only through her teachers' eyes can the principal see her professional performance objectively—what she is doing right, and what she needs to change. With such detailed evaluations in hand, only the most defensive of principals would refuse to consider implementing their suggestions. Yes, it hurts to be criticized, but it hurts even more to be ineffective. When a majority of his faculty told a principal they felt cut off by his isolating himself in his office, he scheduled weekly town meetings for the school population aimed at running the school with renewed vigor. To the faculty's surprise, the principal admitted that he, too, had felt cut off.

HOW?

Just as teachers must have anonymity on student evaluations, so must principals on teacher evaluations. Most principals go so far as to require that evaluations be not only unsigned but typewritten to further insure anonymity.

The best way for you to institute faculty evaluations of the principal is by approaching the faculty directly. Ask your parent group to contact one of the faculty leaders with the suggestion. The teachers, believe me, will love the idea since it gives them an opportunity to tell the principal what may have been on their minds for years. When they carry the suggestion to the principal, she won't be able to say no, however uncertain she may be. If the teachers don't follow through on your suggestion, get your parent group to give it a try. If the principal blanches, explain that no one but she will see them and that they might contain new ideas she could apply to problems confronting the school.

My favorite comment came from a teacher who had been with me in a school for several years before I thought to ask for evaluations. In answering my request for both positive and negative comments, she began, "The good news is that you asked for these comments. The bad news is that you didn't do it years ago."

50 *Try to get the administration to institute a faculty merit system.*

WHY?

Able teachers have been drifting away from the classroom for some years. One reason is that the pay is low; they often can get double or triple their salary in administration or in the business world. During my twenty years of interviewing finalists in the National Teacher of the Year program, I saw one winner after another leave teaching for a higher-paying job; how ironic that the best teachers never saw a classroom again! Another reason for the teacher exodus is that the job gets harder and harder—more drugs, more violence, more bureaucratic and legal restrictions.

While with today's high unemployment teachers are not quick to give up their jobs, they are as quick as their years of service allow to demand transfers from troubled urban schools to easier classrooms in rural and suburban areas. The result is fewer veteran teachers in the areas where they are needed most.

A system of merit pay not only can keep good teachers in teaching but also can keep them teaching where they are needed most. Business has always operated on such a system—promoting the best employees and enhancing their job satisfaction by paying them more for their outstanding contributions to the success of the company. Although unions at one time kept salaries level regardless of teacher worth, they, too, are now open to change.

With merit pay, a teacher has a further incentive to work harder and do a better job, just as a low-level corporate manager has an incentive to become a middle manager and a top manager. Unlike the business executive, however, the teacher ideally will not be encouraged to aspire to the top administrative job, because a teacher performs in the classroom; when she leaves the classroom, she is no longer a teacher. To get the best from her and to do the best for her, schools have to reward her not by promoting her to principal or some other administrative job, but by generously compensating her precisely for being an excellent teacher. The new teacher starts on the low rung, advancing along union pay scales. If she remains adequate, she gets the bar-gained-for pay increments; if, however, she turns into a great teacher, she gets a lot more money. That's merit pay.

Some schools assign the title "master teacher" to their stars and rationalize their higher salaries by asking them to serve as mentors to young teachers. Others just admit these teachers are worth more to the school and simply pay them more. In any case, more schools are using merit pay to hang on to their best teachers, and it is working—in, for example, the Houston Independent School District; the Los Angeles Unified School District; the Dallas Independent School District; the King William County Public School District in Virginia; Tennessee's Cheatham County Central High School; Red Mountain High School in Mesa, Arizona; Sunnyside High School in Tucson, Arizona; and Riverside High School in Greer, South Carolina.

HOW?

The principal of your school is not in a position to institute merit pay. Your parent group will have to tackle the district superintendent of schools to bring that about. She in turn has to convince the teacher unions, which will not be quick to adopt the idea. Remember, they receive membership dues from all teachers, the best as well as the worst, and have the job of assuring them all a fair deal. Caring as the unions do about the welfare of education, however, which in the long run protects all teachers, they may be open to discussion; and with the awareness that more pay for better teachers is a fair deal, they may be open to persuasion.

The biggest stumbling block in selling merit pay is the question, Who decides who's best? The answer should be "Students," since they know better than anyone, but their opinions are often colored by the marks they get. So it's usually administrators who make the decision, often based on tests. Although at present merit evaluation doesn't go much beyond that, it is my hope and that of many educators that a more meaningful system will emerge nationally.

51 *Don't wait for students, parents, and members of the community to offer volunteer help; get the principal to actively enlist it in every area that needs reinforcement.*

WHY?

Volunteer help is, as the saying goes, money in the bank. The principal who puts parents to work as tutors, students as custodial helpers, and members of the community as teachers provides remedial help, keeps the building in good shape, and is able to offer courses other schools have had to drop. Like manufacturers' coupons at the supermarket, volunteers buy him a bargain.

HOW?

Don't let the principal sit back and wait for people to volunteer; he'll be more successful if he takes the initiative. First of all, with the prevalent laissez-faire attitude of most people, few are going to volunteer on their own. Second, when the principal reaches out to people for help, the ego strokes he gives and the do-good feelings he generates are effective persuaders. However, the greatest persuader may be the volunteers' realization that although their votes and taxes aren't doing much to help education, the time they give to the school may do a lot to help their kids.

The principal can enlist volunteers by explaining his needs at group gatherings—PTA or PO meetings, student assemblies, community get-togethers. Since the written word stays around longer than the spoken word, he should follow up his plea with letters and notices.

The school should treat volunteers not only with courtesy but with professionalism. Never should they be allowed to feel like second-class citizens of the school community; rather, they need to be made to feel like major contributors. Schools have achieved this goal in different ways: some send volunteers letters of thanks at the end of the term; some give them a party; many get the local media to do a story on them. The most meaningful expression of appreciation comes, however, directly from the children they have helped: "Thank you for being my special helper"; "Thank you for being fun"; "Please thank your kids for letting me borrow you." A volunteer who had worked painstakingly with a dyslexic fourth-grader cried when the child, finally able to struggle through a first-level book, wrote to her, "Thank you for making me a good reader."

52 Convince the principal to give students a greater say in decision making.

WHY?

A few years ago I undertook to discover what students dislike most about school. The elementary schoolers I questioned answered to the effect that teachers are too bossy; those in junior high, that "we can't ever do what we want"; and the high school students, "Who wants to live in a police state?" Each in his own vernacular had said the same thing: I have no control over my life.

Were you to have to spend a day—not a year, as students do—in the average school in America, you would understand their complaint. You would wear what the principal deems appropriate, your hair length or skirt length determined by his tape measure; you would go to and from classes he demands that you take, on the schedule he sets, to the tone of his bell; you would march to an assembly when he wants one, listening to a speaker of his choice; you would do the amount of homework he requires, take the tests he decides on, and be evaluated by his standards; you would take class notes from the lectures of teachers he hires and be disciplined by him for what he designates as misconduct. You would feel like a robot.

Even though wise school administrators are aware of the problem, they are afraid to make changes that would mean turning over a portion of their control to the students. They face a dilemma: they want students to feel they have power and responsibility in shaping their own education but are afraid they will use it unwisely. And they're right: when you give people control—be they students or teachers—they may make decisions of which you don't approve. That's what having control means. As a result, many an administrator promises students decision-making power—a strong student government or a seat on the administrative council, for instance—and then emasculates that power. A student in Tarrytown, New York, explained the situation his principal had created: "'We're going to give you a lot of rope,' they [the administrators] say, "and then they string you up with it."

This need not be the case, however, and is not the case in many schools where principals not only promise students control but also enable them to exert it. These principals allow students:

- To have a seat on the board of education or the board of trustees.

- To have a say in hiring faculty.

- To determine elective course offerings.

- To have full control of the assembly program.

- To take disciplinary action for student infractions of the rules.

- To serve with faculty and administration on a board to handle major breaches of discipline.

- To act as peer counselors to students in trouble.

Control of this kind, which students have been given in certain schools in New York, Oklahoma, Massachusetts, Colorado, Texas, and elsewhere, boosts student morale and, surprisingly, results in some school decisions that make a lot of sense.

HOW?

The best way to convince the principal to turn over some decision-making power to students is for the students to request it themselves. Ask your child to bring the issue up to the student government, which can appoint a committee to investigate the possibility. When this committee approaches the principal, though, it won't succeed with just a vague plea for more control. It will have to be specific about the areas in which students want greater say and convincing as to why they should have it: for instance, "We don't get anything from the assemblies and would like to run them ourselves so we can have programs that speak to our concerns" or "We think students would be much less apt to cut classes or sneak out for a cigarette if they had to face us instead of you for punishment."

What happens in most cases is that the principal agrees to a trial period with certain modifications; maybe she lets students run half the assemblies and mete out discipline for some infractions but not for others. When they prove themselves capable of using their new powers responsibly, she will have no cause to rescind these powers and may even allow them to be extended even further.

53 *Urge the principal to do what's even more important—to give teachers greater decision-making powers as well.*

WHY?

Some call it site-based management; some call it shared decisionmaking; some call it democracy. Whatever the name, this new form of school control is today's hot topic— decision making in which teachers' voices speak with the same strength as administrators'. And why not, ask its advocates (mostly teachers and parents)? Don't teachers know better than anyone else what's best for students? Who, after all, is on the firing line day after day? Preposterous, retort its detractors (mostly administrators and board members). Teachers aren't in a position to make broad educational decisions; their understanding is limited to a single classroom.

While administrators want to hang on to the reins of control, teachers are champing at the bit. When the Gallup poll asked a sample of teachers whether they felt the role of teachers should extend beyond actual teaching, 96 percent stated emphatically, "Yes," with the greatest number voting to include among teachers' responsibilities the allocation of school funds, curriculum development, choice of books, hiring a principal, determining teachers' and administrators' salaries, and scheduling.

By giving teachers a meaningful role in school management, administration says in a loud voice, "You are professionals." Teachers develop a sense of pride in being able to shrug off the old saw that those who know, do, and those who don't know, teach—because their decision-making power announces that they know. Strongly behind this new movement are the unions, which for years battled for teacher professionalism through higher salaries and are now arming themselves to bring their constituents into a management partnership with the establishment.

Schools that have already switched to school-based management (many have included parents and the community as well as teachers) find not only greater pride among the faculty but also wiser decision making in the school. As a teacher in New York put it, "The pool of ideas is much greater. The school doesn't perch precariously on one person anymore."

So effective has democratic management been that New York's education commissioner has urged schools throughout the state to institute such a system by 1994; the National Education Association has established pilot studies in four states, with the aim of extending them to all fifty; and local teacher associations are demanding this kind of management in collective bargaining. No idea has swept the country's schools with such fervor since Mary Calderon, a physician and a dynamic grandmother, introduced sex education in the sixties, and no idea since John Dewey's progressivism has had the potential of restructuring schools so dramatically.

HOW?

If your school has not considered the possibility of school-based management, you have a big job of persuasion ahead of you. Rest assured that the principal, the superintendent, and the board of education know about it, because they won't have been able to pick up the morning paper or open an education journal without reading about it. Unfortunately, you may also rest assured that if they haven't discussed a management change in your school by now, they are less than enthusiastic.

That being the case, you have to get both the faculty and the parent group behind you in organizing a campaign. Let teachers work through their local association and parents through the administration. Start with the principal. If you win him over, go together to the superintendent and/or the board of education. Point out what other schools have done.

∿ In Orange County, Florida, a group called the Teamwork Approach to Better Schools persuaded the local superintendent of schools to let the group investigate elementary, junior high, and high schools for needed improvements. Acting on its findings, the superintendent instituted new methods of teaching study skills, new kinds of incentives for teachers, and classes for them in decision making.

- In Seattle, teachers gained control of allocating money for services such as a psychiatrist, a school nurse, and additional teachers.

- In Denver, teachers are on the way to making decisions on school budgets, scheduling classes, and interviewing candidates for jobs.

- In Memphis, team decisions include the allocation of resources and staffing.

- In Chaska, Minnesota, teachers serve on a review board to award grants.

- In Marshalltown, Iowa, teachers make key curriculum decisions.

- In Rochester, New York, where all fifty schools have established site-based management (which includes parents), the administration is sharing decisions on key issues ranging from the lunch menu to the hiring of new teachers.

- In schools in Fairbanks, Alaska; Eagle Point, Oregon; Indianapolis, Indiana; Beaverdam, Virginia; Trenton, New Jersey; St. Paul, Minnesota; Fairdale, Kentucky; Greece, New York; and Bellevue, Washington, teachers are being treated like the professionals they have always been: they are deciding what's best for students.

If the administrators in your school and your district have any doubt that democratic decision making is the wave of the future, read them the words of the executive directors of the National Education Association, the National Association of Elementary School Principals, and the National Association of Secondary School Principals:

The bond that unites teachers and principals is a shared dedication to the idea of excellence in every school and quality education for every student. Achieving this goal is never easy. But it is possible when teachers and principals work together in a spirit of collegiality, with mutual respect for their respective professional responsibilities.

54 *Get the principal to establish a room at the school where parents feel welcome.*

WHY?

In speaking to a group of parents in New England recently, I urged them to become more visible in the school. "Great," a mother responded bitterly. "Just explain who's going to see us in the empty auditorium."

"Come now, Liz," another mother joshed. "You know the janitor will." Everyone laughed, and when the joke was explained to me, I realized that the school had no place for parents—not in the building, and not in its philosophy.

By now it must be clear that parents belong in schools: they were their child's teacher long before he went to school; they can lend hundreds of needed hands; and besides, they shell out the money for the schools. It is easy to see why the parents upon whom I urged participation scoffed: their school hadn't caught up to the rest of the country in wanting them there. On second thought, maybe the rest of the country hasn't caught up yet, either; a Metropolitan Life survey reported that 70 percent of teachers think parents view them as enemies. There are, however, many schools that have caught up and want parents to work for them, but have put forth no effort to make parents feel at home. The back of the auditorium, an empty classroom, a corner of the gym—these are the usual meeting places for parents.

One of the most successful parent-school relationships I know of was built over a coffeepot. In an old-fashioned, unfancy elementary school on Manhattan's Lower East Side, parents come and go as familiarly as if they were in their own kitchen. In a way they are, because the school has given them a room of their own. Here they meet to chat; here they wait to pick up children; here they do committee work; and here they keep a coffeepot on the ready. This school across from "the projects" has more parent participation—from mothers who work and grandparents who baby-sit—than I have seen in many schools surrounded by wide green lawns. The school attitude says, "Welcome," and the parents' room says, "You belong."

If more schools would take the simple step of establishing a parents' room, more parents would stop feeling like intruders and begin acting like members of the team.

HOW?

If you can find an unused nook or cranny in the school, you'll have no trouble convincing the principal to let you turn it into a room for parents. Maybe there's an empty office, or part of an office you can partition off; maybe you can find a classroom no longer in use or—as parents of one school found—an old storeroom in the basement. When you do find a place, take a weekend to paint it. Get parents to donate furniture—comfortable chairs, a card table or desk, curtains. Chip in to buy a large coffee maker and take turns supplying the coffee.

When the room is finished, send notices home to parents inviting them in. If you don't get a strong response, ask class mothers and fathers to follow up with phone calls. Ask the janitor to open the room early in the morning and keep it open till dinnertime so that parents have access before and after work. Your parent organization and the school as a whole will reflect the new feelings of warmth and rays of support that emanate from that small room.

55 *Suggest that the principal let the community use the school building after school hours and on weekends.*

WHY?

For years schools stood in American towns and cities amid small houses and large apartment buildings, surrounded by lawns and sidewalks, and while it was the focal point for children and the chief concern of parents, it towered like a fortified bastion above the community. For the community members it could just as well have been surrounded by a moat, so little access did they have to it. As a result, school and community were in frequent conflict over noise, parking, traffic, and harassment, with issues of drugs, crime, and prostitution taking the lead in recent years. Like dogs and cats or teenagers and their parents, school and community seemed natural enemies.

Wise school administrators now realize, however, that the best way to resolve and appease ill feelings in the community is to make the school a part of it: drain the moat, tear down the fortifications, and invite the public in; let the school become a community center.

For years before I arrived, the school I ran had isolated itself from the community behind locked doors and alarm systems, summarily turning down any request for use of the building with an array of excuses ranging from "They may steal something" to "It'll cost too much to keep the lights on." Hostile feelings from the neighborhood permeated the school until one day a young man asked me whether he and some friends could use our gym for a basketball game. To the preconditioned horror of my associates, I said yes, and, as Robert Frost wrote, "that has made all the difference."

From then on the basketball team used the gym once a week; political candidates held preelection debates there; a church group met there for religious instruction; and anyone in the neighborhood who needed a gathering spot knew one was available at the school. It did cost a little extra money to pay the janitor for locking up late and to keep the lights burning overtime, but we didn't pay those expenses; the community groups did. We got extra protection from the police, who were grateful to have a community center of sorts, and a friendlier relationship with our neighbors.

My school certainly was not alone; schools all over have opened their doors to the community—for use by amateur theater groups and senior-citizen book clubs, for sports, and for meetings of clubs and teenage self-help groups. Some schools have gone even further by sharing their facilities with local nonprofit agencies:

- In New Haven, Connecticut, schools and city share a pool, gymnasium, and auditorium.

- The eighteen elementary schools in Boston share their buildings with a senior-citizen high rise and several social-service agencies.

- The city of Wichita, Kansas, and the school district share a library.

Why not your school?

HOW?

First, persuade the principal that bringing the community into the school is to his advantage. Then let the community know that the doors are open—but not through public notices, which might bring on a deluge. Instead, use word of mouth. Parents can alert organizations to which they belong, and the principal can give a simple yes to the next request he receives.

56 Now that you've let the community in, suggest that the school rent out space in off-hours.

WHY?

Small local enterprises are always looking for space to rent, and a school can end their search: the building is accessible, the school environment is suitable, and the price is lower than that of comparable space elsewhere. As for the school, in renting a room or two on weekends or after school hours, it brings in a few extra, always-needed dollars and serves the community as well.

HOW?

The best way to find someone to rent space in your school is to begin with an organization to which one of the parents or children belongs—a dance or music group, Smokenders, or a weight-reduction program, for instance. Get the parent organization to persuade the principal to let the group rent a room. With a parent belonging to the group and the parent organization behind it, the principal will have little reason to turn down the request. When he is able to buy some new books for the library or paint a peeling classroom with the check he receives, he will have even less reason to turn down further requests.

In some school districts, the mom-and-pop business of renting space has grown into a big operation. Montgomery County, Maryland, for instance, takes in tens of thousands of dollars a year by renting public-school space to private schools. School districts in cities such as New York and the Minneapolis suburb of Edina are taking on the role of a major realtor, leasing empty school buildings to apartment and retail complexes.

In order to accomplish large goals such as these, you'll have to work through the school superintendent. I suggest you start small: present the principal of your school with the idea of leasing out space. And here's a word of caution: don't suggest renting space to any group you either don't know or can't check up on through your better business bureau or consumer-affairs department, and don't suggest renting to any organization that will create a stir among parents, such as a drug-rehabilitation program.

57 Urge the principal to invite the community to share in school programs.

WHY?

Schools provide a wealth of entertainment for those fortunate enough to be aware of it—plays, concerts, art shows, science fairs, lectures, dance performances, panel discussions, and so forth. Unfortunately, the audience usually consists only of proud parents and prouder grandparents, who are invited through a flier brought home by their child; if the child is not performing, the flier might remain in his backpack.

The responsibility for these limited audiences rests with the school population, who believe that since it's only a school performance, no one else is interested. Wrong. Many school programs are at such a level that they can compete with local amateur groups, and some are far better. Greenwich High School in Greenwich, Connecticut; the high school in Newton, Massachusetts; and the Master's School in New York's Westchester County, for instance, put on plays and musicals that are close to professional quality. Other schools schedule speakers that local residents would otherwise get to see only on television: an actor appearing on Broadway, an author straight from "Today," a geneticist from Harvard, Magic Johnson, even the president of the United States—all have been guest speakers at schools.

A principal can do a great public-relations job by making an all-out effort to get her community into the school for these programs. In attendance at the last Master's School play were mothers with children, kids from other schools, old people, and couples new to the neighborhood. "I bring my family to all the programs here," a mother told me. Why not? The performances are good, the price is right (free at Master's and under ten dollars at other schools), and transportation is easy in the city, a parking space available elsewhere.

HOW?

Try to turn your principal into a P.R. person. Convince her that your school's programs and performances are too good to be limited to school audiences and that she can create a great image for the school by getting other people to see them.

In order to inform the public, let students make posters to put in local store windows; have them design a flier to drop at front doors in town. Ask the principal to contact the local media for publicity: the newspaper will probably do a story if she gives them an angle, and the radio station might even let the cast of a play sing or act out a scene to alert listeners.

Before the performance, the principal should publicly express her pleasure in having members of the community present and her hope that they will continue to share the school's offerings. Some schools, like the Master's, serve punch, coffee, and cookies afterward to give the audience a chance to talk to each other and to the performers, and to give the principal a chance to make points for the school.

58 *Urge the principal to enlist volunteer teachers from the community.*

WHY?

Every community across the country is a source of teaching talent waiting to be tapped. Urban and suburban schools are surrounded by businesspeople in mammoth corporations and small local stores and services, by people in the arts, science, politics, publishing, social services, communications, marketing, fashion, food—in all the professions whose wheels turn our country. (In all but one, that is—agriculture. Rural schools have the advantage there, plus most of the other resources on a smaller scale.) These people know their work by *doing* it; the rest of us know it only by *reading* about it.

When "the real thing," as one student says, stands before a class, teaching comes alive because the outsider brings the firsthand air of his world into the secondhand learning experience. In cities like Lexington, Kentucky, suburbs in Westchester County, New York, and rural communities as small as Hugo, Oklahoma, people know this and act on their knowledge. Everyone comes out on top: students learn from a new viewpoint; the school enriches its curriculum; and community volunteers discover the thrill of lighting up the darkness.

HOW?

The principal has to look around his school, talk to teachers, students, and parents, and decide what needs to be brought in from the outside. Someone to direct a play? To initiate an environmental program? To talk about business careers? Someone from Russia or Africa or Asia to re-create his culture? A social worker to paint a picture of problem areas? A member of a minority group to share hope for solutions to minority conflicts? A writer to teach writing? An artist to teach art? A builder, a doctor, a union boss, a politician?

Next the principal has to make an appointment with the individual or with an executive of the organization he wants to tap. A parent with personal contacts will help, and if the principal is lucky, a parent may actually be the volunteer he hopes to enlist. He'll probably have more success if he begins by asking her just to speak to a class or to conduct two or three discussions; after she has done this, the idea of teaching a class once a week for a term won't be so apt to overwhelm her.

59 Urge the hiring of more minority teachers.

WHY?

One of a teacher's most important jobs is to stand before his class as a role model. From the first days of kindergarten, when a child sees "my teacher" as the font of all wisdom, until years beyond graduation, we cling to the image of our teachers, not for what they taught us, but for what they were. Long after we have forgotten history dates and literary authors, we remember, "He was tough but fair"... "She had some sense of humor"... "She never lost her temper"... "He really made me feel special." A good teacher is a part of what a child becomes, and, much as I hate to believe it, a bad teacher plays that role, too.

Schools, by hiring a diverse faculty, provide role models that teach lessons denied students in monochrome schools— and I'm not referring only to color. Children should have the privilege of teachers from every minority group—including African Americans, Hispanics, and Asians, Jews and Muslims, the foreign-born, and the handicapped. A New York school's best history teacher is blind; one of the most gifted English teachers I know of coped for years with being manic-depressive; and a sixth-grade class supported its teacher through the worsening symptoms of multiple sclerosis.

Who benefits from a diverse faculty? Black, Puerto Rican, and Vietnamese children? The Jew in a WASP suburb? The kid from a Polish family? The disabled? Yes, of course. In the accomplishments of a teacher with whom they can identify, these students see promise for themselves; in the difficulties they and their teacher have had to struggle through, they see someone who understands; in the secret signs of their special world, they and their teacher can communicate.

As vital as minority teachers are to the growth of minority children, they are even more vital to the so-call majority— the white, American-born, English-speaking, bodily whole boys and girls who, in most of our country, live among neighbors who look just like them. Minority teachers dispel stereotypes when children realize they are as individual as everyone else; they make equality a living lesson when children become aware that they have achieved success; and they drive out bigotry as children grow to respect and love them.

HOW?

If your school is like most outside the country's large urban centers and lacks a diverse faculty, you can attempt to bring about a change on two fronts. First, convince your parents' organization that it is important for your children to have teachers from different minority groups. Explain why, trying to overcome parents' fears with calm, rational arguments. Find out from the district superintendent or the state commissioner's office what schools have minority teachers, and take a group of parents to visit their classes. In some sections of the country, winning this battle is going to be a long and hard struggle in which you will have to overcome emotional blocks, not logical reasoning.

The second front is the principal. She will be easier to convince of the need for minority teachers but may hold back for fear of inciting a riot among parents. If you have been successful in persuading even a segment of the parent population, you may succeed in getting the principal to dip into diversity with a small step at first. When parents see that their children are not being destroyed and that the school is not falling apart, the principal may feel secure in taking larger steps.

She may have a problem, though, in finding minority teachers. The handicapped are willing and eager, but studies reveal that racial minorities are reluctant to teach—some because the pay is low and others because they know the pain of school prejudice. However, the army, recently required to cut back its forces, has instituted a new program to retrain soldiers for civilian careers; those who do not want to retire can study at a special school to become teachers. With a high percentage of blacks, and increasingly Hispanics, in the army, more minority teachers will soon be available to schools. A black ex–army sergeant loves the sixth-graders he now teaches. The kids trust him, he says, because he knows the violence and loneliness they encounter. They respond, "He's like a daddy."

60 *Ask the principal to keep the school open till 5:30 or 6:00 on school days.*

WHY?

A recent study indicates that almost 70 percent of American families have working parents—two in traditional families, one in the growing number of single-parent families. This means that when children leave school at three o'clock, they head to relatives, friends, or baby-sitters, or they return to an empty house. Since many parents have no relatives or friends nearby and can't afford baby-sitters on a regular basis, they are left with the uncomfortable option of letting their children stay home alone. Whether this is good or bad for a child even specialists can't decide: on one hand, latchkey children develop a strong sense of responsibility; on the other, they develop social and emotional problems. Whichever view is right—and surely both can be, depending on the child—the scenario when mom and/or dad comes home, played out over a background of tension, exhaustion, and bids for attention, is not conducive to doing homework, nor does it foster nurturing.

At three o'clock on school days something else happens for many children that is not conducive to their doing homework or receiving nurturing: they have fallen behind and leave school with unanswered questions, not knowing how to do the work assigned them. The result that night is a standoff between parental nagging and the child's resistance, a situation I referred to earlier as Homework Hell.

Schools can play a large part in relieving home situations such as these by providing the constructive supervision and extra help children need. For instance, schools in New York City and Waban, Massachusetts, run programs of arts and supervised play until 5:30 every day, and those in Danville, Illinois, and Forestville, Maryland, provide after-school tutoring.

HOW?

Many after-school programs are initiated by the people who need them most—parents. Get your parent organization to speak to the principal about getting one under way in your school. When he expresses his first concern—lack of money to pay teachers and/or a supervisor—suggest that you and he solve the problem as other schools have done: enlist volunteer help. Or get parents to form a co-op to hire and pay people who can expand after-school learning into new areas such as dance, art, carpentry, and so forth. Every day after school, parents and older students are tutoring children who need academic help and guiding those who don't into art activities, reading, and games.

In most cases it is true that a teacher has to be present to get insurance coverage and to convince anxious parents that the program is safe and sound. Where does the money come from? In Waban, Massachusetts, parents chip in a small amount to pay the teacher; Danville, Illinois, and Forestville, Maryland, run their programs through grants; New York City's school system picks up the tab for its programs. Suggest all three possibilities to your parent organization and your principal, and make the decision together.

61 Ask the principal to investigate the possibility of a year-round school.

WHY?

In 1968, when Hayward, California, switched from a traditional ten-month to a year-round schedule, administrators solved problems that still plague most school districts. City officials complaining of school buildings left empty during the summer, useless and vulnerable to vandalism, relaxed. Working parents, desperate over what to do with their children during summer vacation, found a place to keep them. High school students eager to complete their required credits early and graduate into jobs or college had a way to do it. And teachers, always scrounging for jobs as camp counselors or tour leaders during the summer months in order to make ends meet, at last could go on doing what they wanted to do—teach. There were, of course, drawbacks, not the least of which was figuring out who goes to school during June, July, and August.

Schools solved the problem in a variety of ways. Some divided the year into four quarters, requiring students to attend any three of their choice, with the option of choosing a fourth if they sought extra help or wanted to knock off credits for graduation. Others divided the year into six or eight weeks in school followed by three or four weeks off on a year-round basis, with traditional vacations eliminated or cut short.

The good news in the four-quarter system is that students have greater control since they can select when they attend school and how fast they want to get through it—unless, of course, the first-come, first-served system puts them at the end of the choosing line. Even better, as I see it, is that the four-quarter system gives students falling behind in their work an extra three months to catch up. The good news in the weeks-on-and-off system is that students sustain what they have learned, since they are not breaking off for a two-month hiatus of mind and memory. The bad news in both systems is that families find themselves in a chaos of school and work vacations that usually do not coincide, making child care all but impossible.

Recently educational voices in the United States have been heard proposing an imitation of Japanese scheduling, which keeps all students in school for eleven months, thereby increasing learning hours, utilizing school buildings and employing teachers throughout the year, and not interrupting traditional vacation patterns. As a parent and a former teacher and student, I don't like this idea, believing that eleven months is too long a stretch. I suggest that you investigate year-round schools instead.

HOW?

Dr. Charles Bollinger, director of the National Association for Year Round Schools, said in 1991 that 1.3 million students in sixteen hundred schools in twenty-three states would attend year-round schools in 1992. He stands by his prediction today, pointing out that school districts in twenty-three states, from California through Arizona and Texas, from Louisiana and Florida through Virginia and North Carolina, have switched to a twelve-month school year and stayed with it.

If you are interested in pursuing this possibility for your school, check out the following year-round schools: North Branch High School in North Branch, Minnesota; Parry McCluer High School in Buena Vista, Virginia; Olive School in Novato, California; and Salt Lake Community High School in Salt Lake City. According to the *Pacific Sun*, a weekly newspaper in San Rafael, California, "In every place this has been tried, student scores have improved." In addition, you can write to Dr. Bollinger at the National Association for Year Round Schools (P.O. Box 711386, Dept. BHG, San Diego, CA 92171-1386), asking for any and all materials available. If after studying the idea you are still interested, discuss it with your superintendent of schools, who may have further information and an opinion of value.

There is a newer year-round program developing in twenty states under the name Twenty-first Century Schools; it is aimed at solving the child-care problems of working parents with children aged three to thirteen. The program keeps children in school all day, serves them two meals a day, and charges parents on a sliding scale to supplement state funding. Dr. Matia Finn-Stevenson (Bush Center, Department of Child Development and Social Policy, Yale University, New Haven, CT 06520) is the person to contact.

If by now you are a convert, take the year-round idea to your parent group for consideration of the pros and cons you have come across during your investigation. With parent support, you may have the persuasive clout to get the superintendent or commissioner to set up a year-round system in your school on a trial basis. Although they may seem like a long shot, year-round schools could permanently change the educational calendar in this country.

PART V
How You Can Involve Your Community

62 *Get the community to make the school an essential part of its life.*

WHY?

A community is only as strong as its schools. Studies show that a good school is the number-one reason families move into a neighborhood; businesses have learned that employees won't relocate unless there is a good school for their kids; and local stores can't keep help unless the nearby school is such that it won't provide druggies and gangs to harass them. By forming a link with its schools, a community can add to its own safety and status, putting the tax dollars of its residents to its own advantage as well as theirs.

Last year, 65 percent of students from grades one through six attended school in districts to which businesses contributed a total of almost a billion dollars in cash, materials, and services. If business involvement in school operations does not continue to halt deterioration and encourage reform, America's public education system may give way to private entrepreneurs. Chris Whittle, creator of The Edison Project to reshape American education, for instance, has plans in the works for a thousand profit-making schools, and cities in Texas, Maryland, and Florida have already leased contracts for school management to private companies.

HOW?

Get the PTA or PO to visit local community leaders—retailers, religious leaders, police and firefighters, restaurant managers, museum directors, librarians. Let them know that you consider the school a vital part of the community and feel it would be mutually beneficial to have the community become a vital part of the school.

- Invite these people to visit the school. Have the children present a program about the school and let them make and serve refreshments.

- Give them examples of successful school-community collaborations: in Pierson, Florida, local farmers work with the science department; in Louisville, Kentucky, businesspeople get into the classes and teach; in Ellijay, Georgia, the justice department, the police, and social-service organizations work with teachers and problem students; in Lake Charles, Louisiana, a local television station helps kids produce and air an ongoing television show; in Chandler, Arizona, the community helps students set goals and make career choices; in Tulsa, Oklahoma, over two hundred engineers awaken kids to math and science with Mr. Wizard–type magic; in Cougar Valley, Washington, the Tandy Corporation has formed a partnership with the local elementary school; in Cincinnati, Ohio, a business group has restructured the school system; and in schools throughout the United States, RJR Nabisco has spent thirty million dollars to spur innovative teaching.

↳ Develop ongoing programs to build and reinforce school-community relations. The Education Association of Sparta, Tennessee, for example, has provided its schools with a handbook of community resources and has staged a number of community activities, such as a "Friends of Education Banquet," a "Business and Industry Week," and a "Get Acquainted with Elected Officials" party. Maybe your community will be as fortunate as Chicago, which boasts a corporate executive who presents one teacher a year with a Golden Apple Award—a sum of money and a half year off for professional development.

63 *Get a local business to adopt your school.*

WHY?

When a company adopts a school, it becomes part of a two-way no-lose situation: the school gets support in the form of teachers from "the real world," equipment it needs but can't afford, and involvement outside its confining walls; the company gains a better-educated pool of future employees, a good school for its employees' children to attend, and the reputation of caring about its employees and their community. The populations of the school and company grow from their exposure to each other both as people and as examples.

Two years ago a group of chief executive officers from leading corporations gathered with an equally prestigious group of educators, brainstorming to find ways to improve America's schools. Although educators don't need further proof of their failure, the executives emphasized bitterly the forty billion dollars they have to spend each year on basic education for their workers, who, they pointed out, are graduates of the educators' high schools. The outcome was a partnership between business and schools that has grown to include about 140,000 businesses that give money, goods, and/or services to an equal number of schools—businesses such as IBM, AT&T, Xerox, Nike, Citibank, Apple, State Farm Insurance, and Texaco, among many others.

Successful in their fields, executives demand the same bottom line from the schools they adopt. The CEO of Basic American Foods urges businesses to insist that schools change in order to hold up their end of the partnership, and the chairman of a large New England real-estate development company refused to make further contributions until the school his firm was sponsoring demonstrated reform.

School adoption is not undertaken just by corporations, however. The former chairman of Marion Merrell Dow has adopted Westport High School in Kansas City, Missouri, as a private undertaking, providing college money for graduates, weekend tutoring classes, and teacher workshops. Similarly, an investment banker and a stockbroker have individually adopted two schools in New York City's Harlem.

HOW?

As you build links between the school and the community, you will find some of them to be stronger than others. A small retailer lacks the personnel to help a great deal; city organizations are forbidden by law to go beyond a certain point; social-service groups lack funds. Your best bet, therefore, is a large business or industry that serves the public. As the company gets to know your school more closely and you draw upon its resources, introduce the adopt-a-school idea. Kentucky's Teacher of the Year a few years ago introduced the idea to Louisville's business community and soon had executives in and out of the high school with the familiarity of staff members. The Chicago Board of Education initiated an adopt-a-school program with the slogan that schools needed "a hand, not a handout." What it got with was thirty-three members of a law firm who served as student mentors and then stayed on to become those students' friends.

64 *Organize a gala school-community day.*

WHY?

Most small towns, big cities, and even neighborhoods like
Little Italy and Harlem in New York City put on fairs, street
markets, and art or health shows that bring the community
together. Schools and communities can combine their
efforts for a similar event—with the same result.

The aim of a school-community day is to let local residents meet students and to let students see firsthand how
the wheels of their town turn. Retail stores, professional
offices, social services, the media, municipal departments,
and business firms invite students to get a closer look at
their operations by talking with executives and staff.

While I have not seen an entire community open its myriad doors to students in an ambitious program such as this,
businesses that have individually opened their doors indicate that it can work. "The kids seemed fascinated," a somewhat jaded publisher noted in surprise. "They asked smarter
questions than my assistant," a discount store manager said,
laughing. For their part, students returned to class spurred
on to new careers. One teacher summed up what they
learned this way: "They discovered there's a lot more to
Baskin-Robbins than ice-cream cones." The most valuable
outcome, however, was a strengthened relationship between
the school and the participating business.

I advocate all-out community involvement because it
would bring large numbers of students and community
members together in a newsworthy splash that the local
media would revel in. While it might produce a few hectic
hours in stores and offices, the learning experienced on both
sides would be worth the inconvenience: students would discover that attention to detail, hard work, and even school
lessons are relevant, and the community would discover that
its dollars and know-how are essential to education. Better
yet, both groups would drop divisive stereotypes: students
would realize that the establishment's not all that bad, and
businesspeople would see that students are not the druggies
and dropouts the media make them out to be.

HOW?

Setting up a school-community day is a long-term project. You have to begin by presenting the idea to the principal, who will probably shout an explosive "Impossible" and try to steer you from his office. Assure him, however, that the parents' organization is willing to carry the ball if he agrees. And he will agree, assuming you won't be able to pull it off. You and the parent group can fool him, though, if you are willing to organize like ants, work like beavers, and think through your approach as wisely as owls:

- Decide whether you are going to involve the whole community (if it is small) or a district within the community (if the community is large).

- Get the name, address, and phone number of each company, store, and service that you plan to include.

- Pick a date; Tuesday is often the least congested business day. Be sure to avoid holidays.

- Assign a committee to talk to the mayor before going any further. It will be hard for him to object, since he will get positive media coverage, will not have to spend any money, and will put his schools in a good light.

- If possible, work through business organizations in your town—Kiwanis, Rotary, Lions. Assign groups of parents to discuss the plan with them, and see whether the organizations will help coordinate their members in implementing the plan.

- Assign parents to contact the businesses you hope to include; each parent should be able to handle four or five in a cluster. The parents have to sell them on the idea, so be sure they are armed with convincing arguments. They also have to reassure the businesses of their willingness to help.

- If you have reached this stage with support from the mayor, business clubs, and local companies, professional people, and stores, you are truly on your way. The next step is to report back to the principal and ask for his help with the faculty.

- You must find out when and how the principal and teachers want to release students for visits.

- Parents now have to go back to the stores and businesses they contacted in order to coordinate the student visits.

- At this point the plans have been laid. They seem far simpler on paper than they will when you actually put them in motion. Coordinating a day like this is a mammoth job. To ensure its success, be patient, prepare yourself for each step, and listen to the needs and concerns of the community members you want to involve.

- To make the most of the day, ask teachers to tie it into their teaching and to follow up in class. Above all, make sure students know how to behave and how not to behave when they make their visits. Have them write thank you-letters to each place they visit.

If you accomplish this feat, you may be among the first, so write it up for an educational journal and send a copy to the national PTA. Not only will you get the credit you deserve, but you may encourage other parent groups in other schools and communities.

65 Demand that local authorities provide adequate security in and around the school.

WHY?

When I was a kid, in what my grandchildren call the olden days, a mother sent her child off to school, confident of his teacher-monitored behavior and of his safety. Today she can be confident of neither. Students are sprayed with machine-gun fire, held hostage in classrooms, raped in lavatories, robbed on stairways. The U.S. Bureau of Justice Statistics reported recently that over four hundred thousand junior high and high school students were victims of violent crime in and around their schools in a six-month period. Less newsworthy but equally devastating to a family are the statistics regarding the number of children killed and injured at school crossings and street corners en route to school.

Just as a good education is the right of every American child, so is a safe way to get to school. Although many children are deprived of both rights, you have a way to reclaim them. School safety is as essential as good teaching and is even more of a community responsibility. Your parent group can take up the cudgel in its defense.

HOW?

Begin with safety around the school. If traffic poses a danger, you can push the police department to take any of three different measures, depending on the seriousness of the situation: (1) have a crossing guard stationed there when school opens and closes; (2) have a stoplight put there if traffic is very heavy; (3) have the street closed to traffic during opening and closing hours if a light is not feasible. Don't let the police convince you that a student monitor with a white belt will provide adequate safety; he won't.

With that problem solved, take steps to secure the inside of the school. Most violent crime takes place in city schools; suburban and rural schools pose less of a threat. Parent patrols at the doors and a visitor sign-in system may be adequate, although a study by the National Criminal Justice Reference Service reports that these measures cut school crime by no more than 2 percent. If your school suffers a crime threat, get the police to station a car in front or, if necessary, have a police officer stand at the door.

Chicago has set an example in its attempt to stem the tidal wave of crime in its schools. Working closely with the schools, the police have developed a program called SAFE— Schools Are for Education—and boast of having cut school shootings to near zero. Their program involves the whole community: 150 cops and 412 unarmed security officers who patrol and check for guns; teachers who are trained in crisis prevention; children who do peer counseling; administrators who identify violent kids early on, set clear-cut standards for behavior, and mete out disciplinary measures for infractions; parents who keep safety watches at violence-prone activities like football games; and local businesses that give employees time off to take part in the school's safety programs.

Police in other crime-prone cities like Los Angeles and Oakland and even in a small town like Cokeville, Wyoming, have begun what they call drop drills—exercises to teach children how to lie flat on the floor during a gunfire onslaught. We have come a long way in the wrong direction since the parents of my mother's generation sent kids off to school fearing only the teacher's ruler on their knuckles or another kid's fist in their eye. Schools can't go back to those days, but they can alert the community to existing dangers and demand that it shoulder a large share of the responsibility for protecting its students.

Make your city an education city.

WHY?

A couple of decades ago, America had given up on its cities: businesses moved out, the middle class fled to the suburbs, empty buildings with broken windows became centers for drugs, and crime lurked in the streets. Today many of those same cities not only are filled and flourishing with new business and giant buildings, but have become tourist attractions: Baltimore with its new waterfront, Philadelphia with its parks and restored brownstones, St. Louis, Hartford, Chicago, Atlanta, Jackson, and Cleveland. One of the most dramatic economic revitalizations was that of Memphis, Tennessee.

Memphis is now in the forefront of another kind of revitalization, a rebirth of education. When George Bush issued his America 2000 challenge in 1991 in the hope that communities would restructure their failing school systems, Memphis listened. In late October 1991, 750 business, government, and educational leaders met to start the ball rolling, determined not to let their efforts become, as the mayor put it, "a public-relations approach to addressing education reform where nothing happens." A year later, Memphis was making something happen.

Over a thousand other communities have taken up Bush's challenge and are struggling, as Memphis has struggled, to fix their schools for their children. A single school can go a long way toward improving itself, and one parent can spearhead the effort, as this book points out. However, in most cities the problem is bigger than a single school because the system is bigger: the Chicagos and Denvers and Nashvilles outnumber places like Hugo, Oklahoma, and Sherman, Connecticut.

When a community unites in a determined push to improve its schools, disparate groups come together, probably for the first time: rich and poor, black and white, police officer and citizen, young and old, business and city government. Through speaking to and listening to and maybe for the first time actually *hearing* each other, they begin to see one another from new viewpoints. Somewhere along the way they begin to understand each other, and eventually they learn to trust. In the past it was said that schools have the job of preparing kids to live in their community. Today let it be said that the community has the job of preparing schools to offer kids a chance to live where they choose and be all they were intended to be. You can be the beginning.

HOW?

- Send away to your state department of education for a copy of the reform aims of America 2000. Share it with the parents' organization of your school and pull together a group that is willing to push for change.

- Involve the principal, the superintendent of schools, and the board of education.

- Involve the mayor and city departments.

- Involve the Rotary, Kiwanis, Lions, Elks, and other business groups in your community.

- Involve teachers, students, parents, and administrators from all the schools in your city.

- Appoint task forces composed of members from each segment of the community to meet separately to outline what they consider the schools' major problems. Although they can use America 2000 as a guide, they needn't stick to it, but should instead focus on the individual needs of their schools.

- After many meetings and much time, reconvene the combined task forces, which will, after many more meetings and much more time, make decisions: What needs to be changed in the schools? How are we going to make the changes?

- The rest is history—taking the painstaking steps to put these changes into operation.

Birth is difficult—every parent knows that—but we have a strong helpmate in nature, which takes control of the timing and the mechanics. Rebirth is more difficult because we have to take control ourselves, from initial decision to final product. America's schools are failing, and no matter how hard and long and lonely the job of fixing them may be, each of us must make the decision and shoulder the responsibility.

In 1837 Daniel Webster said, "On the diffusion of education among the people rests the preservation and perpetuation of our free institutions." We know today in far simpler language that unless we reform our schools, our children will lose the America they believe in. You began your child's life. You owe that child the full and fulfilled life that a reborn school can provide.

And you don't have to do it alone. Both your state legislature and the U.S. House of Representatives and Senate have education committees that study and propose bills that may directly affect your school. Find out who the members of those committees are by writing to each legislative body. Keep yourself aware of bills under consideration, either through your local newspaper or through ongoing contact with each education committee. Let committee members know either by phone or by letter how you want them to vote, and urge other parents to do the same.

In addition, prior to an election, gather all the information you can on the candidates' stands on education so that you can vote for those who will strongly support schools. Read their speeches. Write to their campaign headquarters. How committed are they to children? To teachers? How do they think public education should be financed? How great a role do they think the government should play in private education? Do they plan to enforce integration? How? What about sex education? Education for the gifted? Special education? Are they concerned about child care? What standards will they establish at different school levels? How will they evaluate students? Teachers? Principals?

Get information on issues that are important to your child and your school. Disseminate it among the parent body. Then vote for the state and national legislators that will make a positive difference.

Hundreds of towns and cities in every state in the country have become America 2000 communities. As such, they have four aims:

1 To improve today's schools—make them better and more accountable.

2 To create a new generation of American schools.

3 To enable adults to go back to school, recognizing that learning is a lifelong process.

4 To make our communities places where learning can happen.

You can learn more about becoming an America 2000 community by calling 1-800-USA-LEARN (1-800-872-5327) or by writing to the U.S. Department of Education, Washington DC 20202-0498. Your school, your community, and America 2000, working together, can redesign education in this country.

Private and business foundations, aware that the future of America begins in schools today, contribute millions of dollars annually to strengthen education. Following is a state-by-state listing of foundations to which you can apply for financial help for your school. Note that I have not included every foundation, but only those that give sizable grants. I have not included foundations that give mainly to private or religious schools. Nor have I included foundations that give only to associations, clubs, or education systems; I have listed only those that give directly to schools. You will find more specific information in your local library's foundation directory.

Although the following foundations are listed by state, many of them approve grants to schools outside their own state:

Alabama: J. L. Bedsole Foundation, P.O. Box 1137, Mobile 36633

Arizona: The Flinn Foundation, 3300 N. Central Ave., Phoenix 85012.

Arkansas: Winthrop Rockefeller Foundation, 308 E. 8th St., Little Rock 72202.

California: The Ahmanson Foundation, 9215 Wilshire Blvd., Beverly Hills 90210.

The James Irvine Foundation, 1 Market Plaza, San Francisco 94105.

Thomas and Dorothy Leavey Foundation, 4680 Wilshire Blvd., Los Angeles 90010.

The Milken Family Foundation, 15250 Ventura Blvd., Sherman Oaks 91403.

John and Dorothy Shea Foundation, 655 Brea Canyon Rd., Walnut 91789.

Colorado: El Pomar Foundation, 10 Lake Circle Dr., Colorado Springs 80906.

Connecticut: Aetna Foundation, 151 Farmington Ave., Hartford 06156-3180.

Charles E. Culpeper Foundation, 695 E. Main St., Stamford 06901-2138.

General Electric Foundation, 3135 Easton Turnpike, Fairfield 06431.

Travelers Companies Foundation, 1 Tower Sq., Hartford 06183-1060.

The Xerox Foundation, P.O. Box 1600, Stamford 06904.

Delaware: Longwood Foundation, 1004 Wilmington Trust Center, Wilmington 19801.

Florida: Knight Foundation, 2 S. Biscayne Blvd., Miami 33131.

Georgia: Bradley-Turner Foundation, P.O. Box 140, Columbus 31902.

Coca-Cola Foundation, 1 Coca-Cola Plaza N.W., Atlanta 30313.

Hawaii: McInerny Foundation, 1000 Bishop St., Honolulu 96813-2390.

G. N. Wilcox Trust, P.O. Box 2390, Honolulu 96813-2390.

Illinois: Amoco Foundation, 200 E. Randolph Dr., Chicago 60601.

Dr. Scholl Foundation, 11 S. LaSalle St., Chicago 60603.

Indiana: Lilly Endowment, 2801 N. Meridian St., Indianapolis 46208.

Iowa: Roy J. Carver Charitable Trust, P.O. Box 76, Muscatine 52761.

Kentucky: The Humana Foundation, P.O. Box 1438, Louisville 40201.

Louisiana: Baton Rouge Area Foundation, 1 American Pl., Baton Rouge 70825.

Maine: The Maine Community Foundation, 210 Main St., Ellsworth 04605.

Maryland: The Abell Foundation, 1116 Fidelity Bldg., Baltimore 21201-4013.

Massachusetts: The Boston Globe Foundation, 135 Morrissey Blvd., Boston 02107.

Island Foundation, 589 Mill St., Marion 02738.

Amelia Peabody Charitable Foundation, 201 Devonshire St., Boston 02109.

Michigan: Ford Motor Company Foundation, The American Road, Dearborn 48121.

Freedom Forum, 108 S. Stewart, Fremont 49412.

W. K. Kellogg Foundation, 400 North Ave., Battle Creek 49017-3398.

Steelcase Foundation, P.O. Box 1967, Grand Rapids 49507.

Minnesota: The Blandin Foundation, 100 Pekegama Ave. N., Grand Rapids 55744.

Cray Research Foundation, 1440 Northland Dr., Mendota Heights 55120.

Dayton Hudson Foundation, 777 Nicollet Mall, Minneapolis 55402-2055.

General Mills Foundation, P.O. Box 1113, Minneapolis 55440.

Minneapolis Foundation, 500 Foshay Tower, Minneapolis 55402.

Missouri: Anheuser-Busch Foundation, 1 Busch Pl., St. Louis 63118.

Monsanto Foundation, 800 N. Lindbergh Blvd., St. Louis 63167.

Nebraska: The Peter Kiewit Sons, Inc., Foundation, 1000 Kiewit Plaza, Omaha 68131.

Nevada: Conrad N. Hilton Foundation, 100 W. Liberty St., Reno 89501.

New Hampshire: The New Hampshire Charitable Fund, 1 South St., Concord 03302-1335.

New Jersey: The Merck Company Foundation, P.O. Box 2000, Rahway 07065-0900.

The Prudential Foundation, 751 Broad St., Newark 07102-3777.

New York: The Aaron Diamond Foundation, 1270 Avenue of the Americas, New York 10020.

Carnegie Foundation of New York, 437 Madison Ave., New York 10022.

International Paper Company Foundation, 2 Manhattanville Rd., Purchase 10577.

Rockefeller Brothers Foundation, 1290 Avenue of the Americas, New York 10104.

North Carolina: The Cannon Foundation, P.O. Box 548, Concord 28026-0548.

Z. Smith Reynolds Foundation, 101 Reynolds Village, Winston-Salem 27106-5199.

Ohio: Greater Cincinnati Foundation, 802 Carew Tower, Cincinnati 45202-2817.

The Cleveland Foundation, 1422 Euclid Ave., Cleveland 44115-2001.

The George Gund Foundation, 1845 Guildhall Bldg., Cleveland 44115.

Oklahoma: The Samuel Roberts Noble Foundation, P.O. Box 2180, Ardmore 73402.

Oregon: Meger Memorial Trust, 1515 S.W. Fifth Ave., Portland 97201.

Pennsylvania: Alcoa Foundation, 1501 Alcoa Bldg., Pittsburgh 15219-1850.

Annenberg Foundation, 150 Radnor-Chester Rd., St. Davids 19087.

The Buhl Foundation, 4 Gateway Center, Pittsburgh 15222.

Westinghouse Foundation, 11 Stanwix St., Pittsburgh 15222.

South Carolina: Springs Foundation, 104 E. Springs St., Lancaster 29720.

Tennessee: Lyndhurst Foundation, 100 W. Martin Luther King Blvd., Chattanooga 37402.

Maclellan Foundation, Provident Bldg., Chattanooga 37402.

Texas: The George Foundation, 207 S. Third St., Richmond 77469.

The Don and Sybil Harrington Foundation, 700 First National Pl., Amarillo 79101.

Hillcrest Foundation, P.O. Box 830241, Dallas 75283-0241.

T.L.L. Temple Foundation, 109 Temple Blvd., Lufkin 75901.

Utah: The George S. and Dolores Dore Eccles Foundation, 79 S. Main St., 12th Floor, Salt Lake City 84111.

Washington: Weyerhaeuser Company Foundation, CHIF 31, Tacoma 98477.

Wisconsin: Milwaukee Foundation, 1020 N. Broadway, Milwaukee 53202.

National education organizations are replete with information and helpful advice that you may want to tap. Many can refer you to local chapters more accessible to you and your school:

American Council on the Teaching of Foreign Languages, Inc. 579 Broadway, Hastings-on-Hudson, NY 10706.

American Educational Research Association. 1230 17th Street, NW, Washington, DC 20036.

American School Counselor Association. 5999 Stevenson Avenue, Alexandria, VA 22304.

Association for Childhood Education International. 11141 Georgia Avenue, Suite 200, Wheaton, MD 20902.

Association for Supervision and Curriculum Development. 125 North West Street, Alexandria, VA 22314.

Council for Advancement and Support of Education. 11 Dupont Circle, NW, Suite 400, Washington, DC 20036.

Council for American Private Education. 1624 Eye Street, NW, Washington, DC 20006.

Council of the Great City Schools. 1413 K Street, NW, Suite 400, Washington, DC 20005.

Institute for Educational Leadership. 1001 Connecticut Avenue, NW, Washington, DC 20036.

International Reading Association. 800 Barksdale Road, Newark, DE 19714.

National Art Education Association. 1916 Association Drive, Reston, VA 22091.

National Association for the Education of Young Children. 1834 Connecticut Avenue, NW, Washington, DC 20009.

National Association of Elementary School Principals. 1615 Duke Street, Alexandria, VA 22314.

National Association of Secondary School Principals. 1904 Association Drive, Reston, VA 22091.

National Association of State Boards of Education. 701 North Fairfax Street, Suite 340, Alexandria, VA 22314.

National Catholic Educational Association. 1077 30th Street, NW, Suite 100, Washington, DC 20007.

National Committee for Citizens in Education. 10840 Little Patuxent Parkway, Suite 301, Columbia, MD 21004.

National Community Education Association. 119 North Payne Street, Alexandria, VA 22314.

National Congress of Parents and Teachers. 700 North Rush Street, Chicago, IL 60611.

National Middle School Association. P.O. Box 14882, Columbus, OH 43124.

National School Boards Association. 1680 Duke Street, Alexandria, VA 22314.

National School Public Relations Association. 1501 Lee Highway, Arlington, VA 22209.

National School Volunteer Program. 701 North Fairfax Street, Suite 320, Alexandria, VA 22314.